November

by David Mamet

A SAMUEL FRENCH ACTING EDITION

SAMUEL FRENCH

FOUNDED 1830

NEW YORK HOLLYWOOD LONDON TORONTO

SAMUELFRENCH.COM

ISBN 978-0-573-69812-5   Printed in U.S.A.   #16124

IMPORTANT BILLING AND CREDIT REQUIREMENTS

The world premeire of David Mamet's **NOVEMBER** was presented by Jeffrey Richards, Jerry Frankel, Jam Theatricals, Bat-Barry Productions, Michael Cohl, Ergo Entertainment, Michael Filerman, Ronald Frankel, Barbara and Buddy Freitag, James Fuld Jr., Roy Furman, JK Productions, Harold A. Thau, Jamie deRoy/Ted Snowdon and Wendy Federman. at the Barrymore Theater in New York City on January 17, 2008. The production was directed by Joe Mantello with the following cast and creative team:

CHARLES SMITH . . . . Nathan Lane
ARCHER BROWN . . . . .Dylan Baker
THE REPRESENTATIVE OF THE
NATIONAL ASSOCIATION OF
TURKEY AND TURKEY PRODUCTS
MANUFACTURERS. . . . . Ethan Phillips
CLARICE BERNSTEIN . . . . .Laurie Metcalf
DWIGHT GRACKLE . . . . Michael Nichols

Costume Design - Laura Bauer
Lighting Design - Paul Gallo
Set Design - Scott Pask
Technical Supervior - Tony Geballe
Company Manager- Bruce Klinger
Stage Manager - Jill Cordle
General Management - Richards/Climan Inc

THE CHARACTERS

CHARLES SMITH
ARCHER BROWN – two men in suits
TURKEY GUY, A REPRESENTATIVE OF THE NATIONAL ASSOCIATION OF TURKEY AND TURKEY PRODUCTS MANUFACTURERS – a man in suit
CLARICE BERNSTEIN – a lesbian
DWIGHT GRACKLE – a Native American

THE SETTING

An office

THE TIME

ONE
Morning

TWO
Evening

THREE
Morning

"After recording the vice or folly of so many Roman princes it is pleasing to repose, for a moment, on a character conspicuous by the qualities of humanity, justice, temperance, and fortitude: to contemplate a sovereign affable in his palace, pious in the church, impartial on the set of judgement, and victorious, at least by his generals, in the Persian War."

Edward Gibbon
The Decline and Fall of the Roman Empire

This play is dedicated to Jeffrey Richards

ACT I

(AT RISE, **ARCHER BROWN** *and* **CHARLES SMITH** *in an office.* **CHARLES** *is looking at a piece of paper.)*

CHARLES. What is this? What is this? One spot in Cleveland One in Cincinnati…Why…?

ARCHER. You see the polls?

CHARLES. What happened to never say die?

ARCHER. I saw the polls.

CHARLES. You saw the polls, how bad can my numbers be?

ARCHER. You broke the machine.

(pause)

*(***ARCHER*** *hands* **CHARLES** *a sheet of paper.)*

CHARLES. Can these numbers be right? These numbers can't be right.

ARCHER. They're right.

CHARLES. Well, then, the hell with the polls. Must we let our lives be ruled by numbers? Dewey Defeats Truman.

ARCHER. Not this time.

CHARLES. Why? Why? We won the first time, Archie. Four scant years. Why have they turned against me now?

ARCHER. Because you've fucked up everything you've touched.

CHARLES. We're a forgiving people.

ARCHER. Time to cash out, Chucky. Sell a couple pardons, call it a day.

CHARLES. Nobody's spending any money on me. That's the problem, Archie. They dint cut me off, I'd be beating the other guy into marshmallow fluff. All I need, I need, some *money*…

9

ARCHER. And an issue.

CHARLES. How about "continuity."

ARCHER. You've fucked the country into a cocked hat.

CHARLES. Yes, but at least I've done *something*. What has the other fella done? Have you thought of that? *That's* the basis of an ad! Get me the committee.

ARCHER. They'll let you keep what you got, put it in your pocket, but they ain't buying any more air.

CHARLES. *(to phone)* Get me the committee.

ARCHER. You're done, Chuck…

    (The phone rings.)

    (to phone) Hello.

CHARLES. Gimme that.

    (takes phone) Barry?…Cathy. Hi. Hon? Hon, can I… Cathy, I can't talk now…

    (to ARCHER) Can my wife take the couch?.

    (to phone) Take, take the couch where, hon…? …Why do you assume we're going home…

    (to ARCHER) Cause she hasn't seen any ads on T.V. And can she take the couch?

ARCHER. No, she can't take the couch.

CHARLES. No, you can't take the couch, hon.

    (to ARCHER) She had it recovered.

ARCHER. It was recovered with taxpayers money.

CHARLES. It was recovered with taxpayers money, Cath.

    (to ARCHER) Can she reimburse the taxpayers?

    And does she get a discount because the couch has been used…Cath…?

    (to ARCHER) Get me out of here…

ARCHER. *(loudly)* Mr. President, Iran has launched a nuclear strike.

CHARLES. What?

ARCHER. Iran has launched a nuclear…

CHARLES. Ca…Cath? Iran has launched a nuclear strike…

    (to ARCHER) Or could she *uncover* the couch, and take the unupholstered couch…

ARCHER. She can't take the couch.

(*A second phone rings.* ARCHER *answers.*)

Hello. Barry, one moment.

CHARLES. *(to phone)* Cath, I have to, Cath, I'll have to call you back. I'm not being cheap, Cath...I'm...I'm, yes, I'm trying to save money, cause WE'RE GOING HOME BROKE, Cath, and we're being bombed by Iran, so I have to hang up.

ARCHER. Why is the couch so important to her?

CHARLES. She wants it for the Library.

ARCHER. The Library?

CHARLES. My Presidential Library.

(*pause*) What are you telling me?

(*pause*) I gotta have a Library. Archie? Don't I have, like, a, uh, a Library, uh, an Exploratory, uh...

ARCHER. No.

(*pause*)

CHARLES. What is it about me people don't like?

ARCHER. That you're still here.

CHARLES. Well, fuck that, doesn't everybody get a Library?

ARCHER. No.

CHARLES. It's not in the Constitution?

ARCHER. No.

CHARLES. Like a lovely parting gift?

ARCHER. No.

(*Phone rings.*)

CHARLES. *(pause)* Cathy's gonna kill me.

ARCHER. *(re: second phone line)* It's the committee...

CHARLES. *(to phone)* Hel...Hello, Barry... "

Where do you find me...? I'm at the White House, Barry. Where are you? "Nantucket." How are *things* out there...?

ARCHER. *(sotto)* He's screwed you on the election. He's holding back funds. Tell him to disgorge the funds.

CHARLES. *(pause)* Barry, look: you've screwed me on the election, I need to disgorge the funds you're holding for my Library.

(to ARCHER*)* What do I mean, "He's screwed me"...?

(to phone) What do I mean, Barry? I'm looking at the time-buys...

(pause) Well, whose decision was that, Barry? "The committee?" Yeah, no, yes, that's peachy, Barry. With the possible exception, YOU ARE THE COMMITTEE. Barry? You...

(pause) Well, who the fuck is the Committee, if not you?

*(*ARCHER *hands* CHARLES *a list.)*

Three spots in Cleveland, two in Minneapp – ...FOR THE WEEK? FOR THE WHOLE FUCKEN WWWW... WHY DON'T I JUST GO OUT AND GET CLOWN SHOES, 'N PUT A RED RUBBER BALL ON MY FUCKEN NOSE, BE...be...because I want to: Fuck that, Barry, because I'm gonna tell you, no I'm gonna tell you why, and you can jolly well sit there. BECAUSE MY FUCKEN QUESTION TO YOU IS A SPEECH THAT YOU, and your fucken shooting party made to me out hunting quail in Bavaria, when someone turned to me and he said, "Chucky, have you read the Three Musk..." Well, it doesn't sound like you're... No, it doesn't sound like you remember, Barry, when someone asked me: "All for one and one for all." You remember that? And all your tame Krauts, and lifting the import tariffs, and "This is our man," and all that happy horseshit...I DON'T *WANT* a... I DON'T... WHAT THE FUCK AM I GOING TO DO WITH A TIME-SHARE IN *ASPEN*? I want to be President..."

(pause)

(to ARCHER*)* "The hat is empty, there are no more rabbits in it."

(to phone) Is this the man I knew? In the snow? In New Hampshire? BARRY, who ruined his fucken shoes going from door to door? Is this the same man?

CHARLES. *(cont.) (pause)* Well, in what way is he different?

(pause) What does that mean? What does that mean? "A good one to lose"? You know who thinks that way? Losers.

(pause) Let's move on. Tell me about the Library. Well: oh, okay. Good. "We have a fund." How much money do we have in my Library Fund...

(pause) Million.

(pause) Thousand?

(pause) Four *thousand* dollars...?

(pause) I CAN'T GO HOME WITHOUT A LIBRARY FOR CATHY...You know that...I should of thought of that when I invaded where? When *I* invaded where? Barr...? Barry, that was your idea...The fuck it was. The fuck it was. The fuck it was, Bar, YES I FUCKEN MIND IF YOU PUT ME ON HOLD...! I am the President of the United States!

(to ARCHER) Where is he? In Nantucket?.

(to phone) Where are you, on Nantucket? HOW ABOUT I GIVE AWAY half of the island to the Micmacs to build their hotel casino. Yes, I can. Yes, I...Yes, I can, Barry. Well, what are you going to do to me?

(pause) That record was expunged,

(pause) That record was expunged, and the statute of limitations...

(pause) Well, who's to say what's perjury...?

(pause; to ARCHER) His friend the special prosecutor.

(pause; to phone) Yeah. Alr...yeah. Alr...Alright...Barry.

(pause) And give my best to Ginny.

(pause; hangs up)

ARCHER. "Life goes on"?

CHARLES. *(pause)* He was gonna put me on "hold."

ARCHER. Everybody goes home sometime, Chucky...

(pause)

CHARLES. Couldn't we make it rain or something, just to keep the other guys from voting...? The other guys stop voting, the incumbent wins, 'int that the rule? Can't we oh, you know, just make it rain...?

ARCHER. We don't have that technology.

CHARLES. In some secret, uh uh...

ARCHER. No.

CHARLES. "Facility," or something.

ARCHER. No.

CHARLES. The panic level: raise the panic level!

ARCHER. Nobody cares.

CHARLES. They don't care about the panic level?

ARCHER. No.

CHARLES. After all our work?

ARCHER. Nobody cares. They hate you. Everybody hates you, and you're out of cash. Go home.

CHARLES. I would hate to think. That the people were deprived of a choice. Because one side...Simply ran out of cash.

ARCHER. That's the American way.

CHARLES. Well, that makes me throw up.

(**ARCHER** *hands him a piece of paper.*)

What is this?

ARCHER. Today's off-the-cuff remarks.

CHARLES. Can't they stick that thing in my ear?

ARCHER. The last one got stuck in your ear.

CHARLES. *(to self)* That's right.

(re: speech) "We must and can and shall move forward" I'm supposed to say this about what?

ARCHER. Whatever they ask you.

CHARLES. How can Bernstein write this crap?

ARCHER. She didn't write it.

CHARLES. Bernstein didn't write it?

ARCHER. No. She's on vacation.

CHARLES. Aha.

> *(pause)* It *almost*: were I of a paranoid *bent*, would make me *opine*. That somebody was out to get me.

ARCHER. I don't follow.

CHARLES. That, one, the committee has ceased spending money on me...

ARCHER. Yeah...

CHARLES. At the same time. As my *speechwriter*. Has chosen to take a vacation. Why?

ARCHER. Your ten o'clock is in the anteroom, with fifty thou...

> *(**ARCHER** hands him papers.)*

CHARLES. Get Bernstein to re-write this crap. Where is she?

ARCHER. She's technically still on vacation.

CHARLES. Get her to write it on vacation.

ARCHER. She's already working on vacation.

CHARLES. What's she working on?

ARCHER. She's working on your concession speech.

CHARLES. OH FUCK THIS FUCKIN LIFE AND EVERY-THING IT *STANDS* FOR. Fucken Bernstein. Sinking ship...

ARCHER. Chuck.

CHARLES. *I* don't get a vacation...

ARCHER. She hasn't had a vacation in four years.

CHARLES. Well, she lives for her fucken work. She hasn't got a family.

ARCHER. She lives with that girl.

CHARLES. Well, they haven't got children.

ARCHER. She went to China to pick up a kid.

> *(pause)*

CHARLES. She went to China to pick up a kid.

ARCHER. She went to adopt a baby...

> *(pause)*

CHARLES. She *went* to *China* to *adopt* a baby.

ARCHER. What's so extraord...

CHARLES. Aren't we at war with China?

ARCHER. Not yet...

CHARLES. Well, it sounds like treason to *me.*

ARCHER. How?

CHARLES. She, after four years. Goes to China, to quote quote complete her *family.* To raise a child. Which she could not DO, if, if I were to serve another term.
(pause) Oh, I begin to see it, I begin to see it: Why does she go now. Yes. Bernstein. Why "now"?

ARCHER. Why now what?

CHARLES. For, it is not her "quote" biological "*clock,*" as she is *buying* the child, so whence this sudden rush of wings?

ARCHER. ...Alright, "whence"?

CHARLES. She GOES TO CHINA, *NOW,* because, she raises the kid NOW, because I'm out of OFFICE. THAT is why it's fucken *treason.*

ARCHER. ...Chuck

CHARLES. To *China.*

ARCHER. *(to phone)* Get Bernstein to come in.

CHARLES. ...The only place you can get a meal on Christmas?

ARCHER. ...Chuck.

CHARLES. ...Chinese restaurant.

ARCHER. ...Chuck.

CHARLES. They're always open. Fucken chinks. They got all the time in the world...and they don't mind working themselves to death...Sell you the ground they walk on, sell the various offspring of their wombs. Fucking Bernstein. Fly'n off to *China,* her vacation. What'd she get, a baby girl?

ARCHER. That's all they sell...

CHARLES. *(reads)* "To boldly address those problems which confront us...with hope..." Who writes this shit?

(phone rings)

ARCHER. Children from Yale.

*(**ARCHER** answers the phone.)*

Yes:

CHARLES. Get Bernstein in.

ARCHER. ...She just got in last night. At three a.m.

CHARLES. Get her in.

ARCHER. She called to say she's sick.

CHARLES. What's she got, "bird flu"?

ARCHER. I think she's just tired.

CHARLES. She's just tired. What is she, "nursing"? Oh. I forgot. She's not "nursing," cause she *bought* the baby.

ARCHER. Your ten o'clock appointment.

CHARLES. Get Bernstein in here. I want to *confront* her treasonous ass. One thing I've learned in this job, Arch?

ARCHER. Yes.

CHARLES. One *thing...*?

ARCHER. Yes.

CHARLES. Is who can you trust?

ARCHER. You can trust me, Chucky.

CHARLES. Apart from you.

ARCHER. Nobody.

CHARLES. *This* broad: one, bails out, two, writes my *concession* speech, three, THREE? Where does she go to *write* it?

ARCHER. China.

CHARLES. Do the math. And pee fucken ess: What in the world, do you think, all these cute lil Chinese baby girls are gonna do, when they grow up, having eaten our food, learned to play the cello, bested all the white children at math, and slurped up all the jobs, under affirmative action.

ARCHER. Chuck...

CHARLES. And looked over the water, at their HOME-LAND, the preeminent nation in the world.

ARCHER. We're the preeminent nation in the world.

CHARLES. For how long? Until the All-Star break? AND NOW THEY LOOK AROUND, THESE LITTLE FUCKEN BENEDIK ARNOLDS, seeded, *seeded* here…

(The phone rings.)

ARCHER. *(to phone)* Yes…?

CHARLES. By a *wily* Oriental nation.

ARCHER. *(to phone)* I'll tell him.

CHARLES. Cause they don't count time, like we do. Arch. Have you noticed this? The Chinese? A thousand years is as a single day to them.

ARCHER. I think that's to God.

CHARLES. No, it's the Chinese. They can *wait.* They can afford to wait. They got nothin but time. I'm out of time.

ARCHER. *(of phone)* The National Association of…

CHARLES. Where did I go wrong?

ARCHER. You lost the election…

CHARLES. Not *yet* I haven't.

ARCHER. Take the money, and go home. Sell a buncha *pardons…*

CHARLES. I should sell pardons…

ARCHER. Yes.

CHARLES. …how many people, are both "guilty," Arch, and have the money…?

ARCHER. Quite a few. *And*: under the statute, you have until the election to accumulate quote quote campaign funds.

CHARLES. *(to phone)* Get fucken Bernstein in here.

ARCHER. Any of which, unspent, you can retain for your personal use. For *instance*:

CHARLES. *(to phone)* Well, send my protective detail for her. What do you *mean* they have the morning off? They only work a half *day* today? *Why? Cutbacks?* What're we spending all the *money* on –

(pause; to phone) Oh – Well, send the *Marines.*

(pause) Well, where *are* the Marines?

(pause) All of them...? Is this generally known?

ARCHER. I fucken hope not.

(hangs up)

CHARLES. Who is my ten o'clock?

ARCHER. National Association of Turkey Manufacturers.

CHARLES. What do they want?

ARCHER. To pardon their turkey.

(pause)

CHARLES. What did it do?

ARCHER. It's a promotional thing.

CHARLES. And now they want me, these fucken "turkey" people, to "pardon" their turkey...

ARCHER. They want you to come out.

CHARLES. To come out where?

ARCHER. In the anteroom.

CHARLES. Why?

ARCHER. The turkeys want to smell your hand.

(pause)

CHARLES. You want me to go into the outer office, to let a turkey smell my hand?

ARCHER. Two turkeys.

CHARLES. *(pause; to self)* The President of the United States...

ARCHER. They're very sensitive.

CHARLES. Well, so am *I.* So am I, Archie...

ARCHER. ...so that tomorrow *morning,* when you come out, and pardon them...

CHARLES. ...and this is what my job comes down to.

ARCHER. You did it the last three years.

CHARLES. What did they pay me?

ARCHER. The usual.

CHARLES. Which is?

ARCHER. Fifty grand.

CHARLES. "Turk-*eez*," you said.

ARCHER. The regular, and an alternate.

CHARLES. Last year. Ah. Yes. I pardoned *one* turkey.

ARCHER. This year they have two.

CHARLES. ...why do they have two?

ARCHER. Last year the turkey got sick, they were concerned it would die. And, so, this year they have a head turkey and an alternate.

CHARLES. And *what* did they pay me last year?

ARCHER. The same fifty grand.

CHARLES. Fifty grand, but this year, they have two turkeys.

ARCHER. That's right.

CHARLES. So, the going rate, *this* year...fifty grand a pop... would be not *fifty*, but *a hundred* thousand dollars.

ARCHER. I'm not sure that they've got it in them.

CHARLES. Well, lets find out – How much is turkey?

(to phone) How much is turkey a pound? No, tell her I'm busy.

(pause) Yeah, alright. Cathy: we're not at war with Iraq. I misspoke...

ARCHER. We are at war with Iraq.

CHARLES. Cathy? We ARE at war with Iraq, we AREN'T at war with Iran.

(pause) I'll tell you when...

(hangs up phone)

(The intercom rings. ARCHER answers it.)

ARCHER. Yes. Turkey is a dollar ninety eight a pound.

(He hangs up.)

CHARLES. Turkey is a dollar ninety eight a pound...

ARCHER. Yes.

CHARLES. Alright: suppose. Three hundred million people. Knock out fucken half of them, uh, the old, the young, uh babies, vegetarians, uh...

ARCHER. The homeless.

CHARLES. If each American left, simply eats one, ONE pound of turkey…knock off two-thirds, you've got a hundred million people. One pound at two bucks a pound. How much is that?

ARCHER. Two hundred million dollars.

CHARLES. That is two hundred million dollars. And these *little rascals*, waltz in here with fifty grand. While my *wife*, Archie, weeps at home "can she recover the couch?" Get me the speech broad. I got something to say.

ARCHER. She's home sick.

CHARLES. I don't care if she's dead. Fuck *her, all* of her brilliance.

ARCHER. She's sick, Charles.

CHARLES. I don't give a f…*Gimme* that fucken…Get me my speechwriter.

(He grabs for the phone.)

*(**ARCHER** takes the phone.)*

ARCHER. *(to intercom phone)* Send a car, please. Call Ms. Bernstein. We need…

*(to **CHARLES**)* Why do we need her to come in?

CHARLES. Because I *say* so.

ARCHER. *(to phone)* A matter of grave national importance.

(hangs up phone)

CHARLES. Tell her in *her* words, "Our capacity is only bounded by our dreams." In *her words.* So she can just fucken bite the bullet.

(The phone rings.)

ARCHER. *(takes phone, listens)* Can she work at home?

CHARLES. YOU TELL THAT BROAD, YOU *TELL* HER: I AM SICK OF HER THIS IS THE LAST TIMMMME. YOU KNOW WHAT? She ain't in her *chair* ten minutes, I am puttin' her on the *piggy* plane.

ARCHER. Chucky…

CHARLES. The piggy plane. I am not kidding. You think I'm kidding? Look in my eyes. AT HER DOOR, someone will be at her door.

ARCHER. Chuck…

CHARLES. With manacles, and what? A bag over her head. Lest she scream, and a *Lear* jet…

ARCHER. Chuck…

CHARLES. To whisk her on the piggy plane to Prybschych, Bulgaria, to spend the rest of her life as an enemy combatant. How about that?

ARCHER. Chuck…

*(The phone rings. **ARCHER** answers.)*

CHARLES. Because, Arch. If I have to spend. Each moment of my working day, *explaining…*

ARCHER. Chuck…

CHARLES. Cajoling, reassuring, and *supervising* the work I would have assumed *done*, then…

ARCHER. Chuck.

CHARLES. Then, it's time for a change.

ARCHER. Chuck.

CHARLES. I know what everybody thinks. Chuck Smith. Who is he? He's an empty suit. Ha ha. Let him indulge his penchant for…

ARCHER. …Chuck…

CHARLES. …for "rhetoric," for "bombast." Isn't it cute how he…

ARCHER. *(of phone)* Chuck. It's the guy from Iran.

CHARLES. …takes everything to heart. Old grandpa. Hyuh, hyuh, hyuh.

ARCHER. *(of phone)* It's the guy from Iran.

CHARLES. Put his ass right on hold.

(pause)

*(**ARCHER** starts to speak.)*

No. I will deal with him in due course.

(pause) I would like a cup of coffee. When Ms. Bernstein appears, disinfect her, as I do not wish to acquire, whatever cooties she's contracted on the *plane*....take a breath and listen to me.

(pause) Things. From now on. Will, in their running, more closely approximate a Swiss watch, and less and less call to mind A CLUSTER FUCK. I'm too old. I'm too tired. And, if "things" don't, heads are going to roll. Arch. Heads are going to roll. And where they come to rest, I do not care.

(A second line rings. ARCHER answers.)

ARCHER. The Turkey and Poultry Association.

CHARLES. To review, *yes*? How much is turkey a pound...?

ARCHER. It's a dollar ninety-eight.

CHARLES. Two dollars. And so. One hundred million people eating, each, one pound would be...?

ARCHER. Two hundred million dollars.

CHARLES. Now. Let the chucklehead waltz in here with his fifty grand. Show him in.

ARCHER. Iran's still holding.

CHARLES. Arch. Theodore Roosevelt sat in this chair. Do you know what his policy was?

ARCHER. No, Chuck.

CHARLES. In a word. His policy was "How about that?" Show the turkey people in. Gimme his card.

(The TURKEY GUY comes in.)

(ARCHER hands CHARLES a card.)

(CHARLES reads it.)

TURKEY GUY. Mister P....

CHARLES. Siddown.

(re: card) You still, what is this...cultivating fighting fish?

TURKEY GUY. Yes, Sir, I...

CHARLES. And how is "Betty?" – Now, we've got *that* out of the way...

(The phone rings. **ARCHER** *answers.)*

ARCHER. *(to phone)* Yes…?

TURKEY GUY. Mister…

ARCHER. *(of phone)* It's that fellow we were speaking of.

CHARLES. *(to* **TURKEY GUY***)* Siddown…

TURKEY GUY. Sir. I cannot express our great sense of…

CHARLES. Get to it.

TURKEY GUY. Honor, and..

ARCHER. We're rather busy.

TURKEY GUY. Yes. Of course, sir. In the past…

CHARLES. Fuck the past. We're going to start anew. Don't
you think?

TURKEY GUY. Absss…

(The phone rings. **ARCHER** *answers.)*

ARCHER. It's the fellow from Iran. He's denying the rumor
that he has launched missiles.

CHARLES. Who told anyone he had launched missiles?

ARCHER. You told your wife.

CHARLES. *Christ* that woman is a gossip…
(*pause)* Tell him it's cool, big mistake, and I'll take care
of it.
(to **TURKEY GUY***)* Now: my friend. I would like to bring
your attention to some simple facts.

TURKEY GUY. Of course, sir.

CHARLES. You ready?

TURKEY GUY. Yes. Sir. I am.

CHARLES. There are: How many people in this country?
(to **ARCHER***)*

ARCHER. Three hundred million, several odd hundred
th…

CHARLES. Say three hundred million. On *Thanksgiving.*

TURKEY GUY. Yes, sir.

CHARLES. How many, would you say, "eat turkey"?

TURKEY GUY. *All* of them…?

CHARLES. That would be yummy, but, let's say, purpose of argument, one hundred million. Zat sound? Fair to all concerned?

TURKEY GUY. Yes, sir.

CHARLES. How much is turkey a pound?

TURKEY GUY. I...

CHARLES. This morning. At the opening bell. Turkey at the supermarket. "Turkey" could be had for...?

TURKEY GUY. Well. Well, sir, I. I don't know, regional discrepancies...

CHARLES. Don't fuck with me.

ARCHER. How much is turkey a pound?

TURKEY GUY. "A" turkey...

CHARLES. Do you know where Prondachzeck, Bulgaria is?

TURKEY GUY. No, sir.

CHARLES. Nobody does.

(pause) Just five guys. Who work for me.

(pause) And the fellas who they *take* there...

(pause) And leave there.

(The phone rings.)

CHARLES. *(to phone)* What?

(to TURKEY GUY*)* It's for you...

TURKEY GUY. Excuse me...

(to CHARLES*)* Yes. *(He listens to the phone, then hangs up and addresses the President.)* Sir, there is a woman in the anteroom, who is sneezing.

CHARLES. How much is turkey a pound?

TURKEY GUY. And could you issue orders that she is to be kept away from the birds?

CHARLES. How much is turkey a pound.

TURKEY GUY. ...for the birds, Sir, have been raised in *complete* isolation, under strictest standards of organic veterinary care...

CHARLES. Yeah, Ok.

TURKEY GUY. And a woman is sneezing in the outer office

CHARLES. *(to phone)* Who's sneezing? Get her in here.

*(**BERNSTEIN** enters, wearing a large, colorful Chinese amulet around her neck. Sneezes.)*

BERNSTEIN. Mister President.

CHARLES. Bernstein.

(She sneezes again.)

TURKEY GUY. Sir, when this person leaves, could you ask her to exit by, a route which will not place her again in proximity to the turkeys?

CHARLES. What is it you want, pal?

TURKEY GUY. Mister President?

CHARLES. Quid pro quo. Quid pro quo. What do you want?

TURKEY GUY. For you to pardon…

CHARLES. Good! You know, many fine folks, grew up comfortable, went to college, nothing wrong with that, I however, was raised in a migrant camp. And one thing that I learned. Is Life? Life is one thing.

ARCHER. Give and take.

CHARLES. Give and fucken take.

TURKEY GUY. Mist…

CHARLES. Give and take. Way the thing lays out? You want something. I got what you want? You give, and I take. Or else you wouldn't be here.

*(re: **TURKEY GUY**) Bernstein?*

BERNSTEIN. Sir?

CHARLES. What do these guys want?

BERNSTEIN. Sir?

CHARLES. Are you sitting down? They want me TO PARDON A TURKEY.

TURKEY GUY. Two turkeys.

BERNSTEIN. Sir, you weren't raised in a migrant camp. You grew up in Shaker Heights.

CHARLES. …And you think that was a picnic?

*(The phone rings. **ARCHER** answers it.)*

What?

ARCHER. It's the Israeli ambassador. "The future of the State of Israel…"

CHARLES. *(takes phone)* What? Iran has not launched…I… Iran has not…

(to ARCHER) Get my wife on the phone…*(to phone)* Iran has…Look: you people, got along without a country for two thousand years. You're gonna be fine. All right? *(He hangs up.)*

(pause)

BERNSTEIN. Sir, my baby…

CHARLES. *(to TURKEY GUY)* This office has not raised its fee for twenty years. One turkey, fifty grand, but, but, you want me now to cut my price in half. And pardon not one, but two…and here's one for you: IS IT A CRIME?

TURKEY GUY. Mist…

CHARLES. Being a turkey? Is it a crime?

TURKEY GUY. Sir, the country understands the gesture as one of, of, of, of "whimsy."

CHARLES. But they, I believe, have overlooked the underlying logic of the case.

(The phone rings.)

ARCHER. *(to phone)* Yes?

(to CHARLES) Chuck…It's your wife.

CHARLES. *(to phone)* Can you keep you trap shut about things that I tell you in confidence.

(He hangs up.) I pardon your turkeys, what does that imply? That the birds I *haven't* pardoned, the turkeys each American actually eats, on Thanksgiving, are criminals?

TURKEY GUY. I…

CHARLES. And you know what, perhaps I do not have the *power* to pardon turkeys.

TURKEY GUY. Sir, Presidents since World War Two have pardoned turkeys.

CHARLES. At what cost.

TURKEY GUY. *(pause)* Sir…

ARCHER. What did you give em?

TURKEY GUY. Sir, if you would like us to consider raising our organization's stipend, to your, your…

CHARLES. Oh good. Now we're getting somewhere. Archer?

ARCHER. Sir?

CHARLES. Do I have the power to pardon turkeys? *Ask* me.

ARCHER. Mister President? Can you pardon turkeys?

CHARLES. Not for one hundred thousand dollars.

TURKEY GUY. One hundred?

CHARLES. Fifty grand a bird.

TURKEY GUY. Alright.

CHARLES. No, I said *not* for one hundred thousand dollars. That's the old price.

TURKEY GUY. Fifty grand was the old price.

CHARLES. Times one turkey. Times two that would be a hundred – That's the old price. Do I hear an increase on the old price?

TURKEY GUY. One hundred fifty thousand.

CHARLES. I don't think so.

TURKEY GUY. One eighty-five.

CHARLES. In cash.

TURKEY GUY. Yes, Sir…

(The phone rings.)

(TURKEY GUY extends his hand.)

(CHARLES checks his info card.)

CHARLES. *(to TURKEY GUY)* Give my best to Betty…

(ARCHER answers, listens.)

ARCHER. *(pause)* Hold the phone.

CHARLES. Yes.

ARCHER. The price of turkey was quoted at two dollars a pound.

CHARLES. Yes…?

ARCHER. That's "on the bird."

CHARLES. What else could it be?

ARCHER. Pre-sliced.

CHARLES. What is it pre-sliced?

ARCHER. Between seven and eleven dollars.

CHARLES. *(to exiting* **TURKEY GUY***)* Stop right there.

TURKEY GUY. Sir?

CHARLES. Let's start again. Seven dollars a pound times three hundred *million* people does not equal, one hundred eighty-five grand.

TURKEY GUY. What does it equal?

CHARLES. You tell me.

TURKEY GUY. You want me to bid against myself?

CHARLES. How *dare* you, employ language like that, in this sacred office.

TURKEY GUY. I beg your pardon. Tell me what you require.

CHARLES. I want a number so high even dogs can't hear it. Are you cogitating?

(pause)

TURKEY GUY. I am.

CHARLES. And where have your deliberations led you?

TURKEY GUY. "No."

CHARLES. "No" – to your Commander-in-Chief?

TURKEY GUY. Yes.

CHARLES. Okay – that's treason.

TURKEY GUY. *Treason?*

CHARLES. Under my wartime powers? You bet your ass.

TURKEY GUY. You know what, I don't *think* so. You know why?

CHARLES. Why?

TURKEY GUY. You're *dead.*

CHARLES. I'm *dead...?*

TURKEY GUY. Your numbers are lower than Gandhi's cholesterol; and, after the election, we'll see you at *Swap Meets* signing autographs. You *LOSER.*

CHARLES. *(to phone)* Get me the Pork People on the phone...

(**ARCHER** *takes the phone.*)

TURKEY GUY. Oh. You're gonna sell "pork" on Thanksgiving.

CHARLES. Watch me. Show this gentleman out...

(**ARCHER** *motions the* **TURKEY GUY** *out.*)

ARCHER. *(on phone)* ...holding for the pork people...

CHARLES. *(pause)* Bernstein.

BERNSTEIN. Sir?

CHARLES. What is that about your neck?

BERNSTEIN. Sir, it is a Chinese amulet.

CHARLES. An "amulet?"

BERNSTEIN. That's right.

CHARLES. From "China?"

BERNSTEIN. Yessir.

(*pause*)

CHARLES. Ah huh...Bernstein?

BERNSTEIN. Sir?

CHARLES. Are you "enamored" of that Oriental Power?

BERNSTEIN. Sir, I am not.

CHARLES. And yet you bear their "mark" about your neck.

BERNSTEIN. Sir, it is a symbol of love.

CHARLES. ...aah...

BERNSTEIN. And Family Unity.

CHARLES. And how am I to know that? Bernstein? I don't read Chinese...Do you?

BERNSTEIN. They gave it to me at the hospital.

CHARLES. Uh huh.

BERNSTEIN. When we went to claim our daughter.

CHARLES. Then you don't *know* what it means...

BERNSTEIN. They told me.

CHARLES. Do you suppose, Bernstein, the Chinese are incapable, of hanging on your neck, a symbol, which said to their cohorts, in *this* country...

ARCHER. I have the Pork People on the phone.

CHARLES. …"Rise up and kill the White Oppressor."

BERNSTEIN. They give it to all families who adopt a child.

CHARLES. What better conduit, Bernstein, for their filth. Can you be so naive?

BERNSTEIN. Sir –

CHARLES. Are you a friend of those forces inimical to the best interests of your native land?

BERNSTEIN. Sir, I am not.

CHARLES. And yet you went to China.

BERNSTEIN. Sir, Nixon went to China.

CHARLES. He went to play pingpong.

ARCHER. National Confraternity of Pork and Pork Product Producers…

(CHARLES takes the phone.)

CHARLES. *(to phone)* Hello, Tink? How they hanging…?

(to ARCHER) Caught between a dick and an asshole. *(to phone)* That's a good one. Tink…

(to ARCHER) Are we calling about that "thing," about the piggyplane…?

ARCHER. What thing about the piggyplane?

CHARLES. Tink, far as I know, we've got a clean board on the *piggyplane*…

(to ARCHER) Some guy in Bulgaria wants to file a complaint to…what? The International Amnesty for Victims of Oppression? They saw the piggy plane? They saw the people getting off the plane? Bags over their heads, in manacles…How'd they know the plane was yours?

(to ARCHER) They saw the curly thing on the tail.

ARCHER. I *told* him not to put that thing on the tail.

CHARLES. Who saw it? A reporter?

(he nods) Tink? Get me his name and we'll have him killed…Tink… Yeah, it's been such fun working with you, *too*…But Tink? Lookit *here*: my *Library*…

(pause; to ARCHER) He was thrilled to be able to make the contribution he made to our…our campaign, and he only wishes it could have been more.

CHARLES. *(cont.)* *(to phone)* Tink: I think I may be able to make your wish come true. Look here: Tink: You sitting down? What if. What if. What if: historically, at Thanksgiving. Americans. DID NOT EAT TURKEY.

(pause) Well, they ate pork.

(pause) Well, who the fuck knows if they did or not. There's guys say World War *Two* never took place.

(pause) I dunno, some *Frenchmen.* Point of my call: Tink. I got these turkey guys, want me to bless their turkeys. But – I'd rather go to my friends:

(BERNSTEIN sneezes.)

Tink, I would like to use the power of my office, to *inform* the American populace that, from now on. We will *not* demean, the memory of our ancestors white *and* red by eating turkey at Thanksgiving, but…hold on, but, BUT will honor them by eating pork.

(pause) Fuck the Jews.

(to ARCHER*)* Do the Jews celebrate Thanksgiving?

ARCHER. How do I know…?

CHARLES. *(listens to phone)* Who?…Well, fuck them, too. How many Arabs do we *have* here…?

(pause) Oh.

(pause) Jeez…

(pause) Well…

(to ARCHER*)* "How about some *other* holiday?".

ARCHER. That's not what we're selling.

CHARLES. *(to phone)* Tink, that's not what we're selling. Tink. Today here's what we're selling: we're selling, on Thanksgiving, Pilgrims ate pork. Pilgrims ate pork on Thanksgiving.

(pause) Well thanks anyway. And "do I want a seat on his Board?"

(ARCHER holds up two fingers.)

No, you know what, Tink. Hey, gimme *two* seats on the Board. You bet. Thanks for listening.

(hangs up) He thinks he "gave" cause he lent us the piggyplane…Sinking ship, sinking ship?

(to himself) They didn't eat pork on Thanksgiving… They didn't eat Turkey…

*(to **ARCHER**)* What about if they ate tuna?

ARCHER. Who?

CHARLES. The American people.

ARCHER. They ate tuna on Thanksgiving?

CHARLES. That's right.

ARCHER. Tuna.

CHARLES. Yes.

ARCHER. Is, I believe, a Pacific fish.

CHARLES. Yeah.

ARCHER. And the pilgrims…

BERNSTEIN. Mr. President, may I go home?

ARCHER. Landed on the East Coast.

CHARLES. Because of the time change.

BERNSTEIN. …Mist…

CHARLES. No, I'm gonna need you, Bernstein. Okay, okay. The pilgrims. They did not eat "tuna…" They ate some species of "codfish," which, the Indians
*(to **ARCHER**)* Find me an Indian…

*(**ARCHER** looks for a card.)*

…in their *ignorance*, called tooohnah, which in the blah blah *language* means "great abundance from the sea."

BERNSTEIN. Mister President, may I go home?

CHARLES. When I'm done with you, Bernstein. When you've fulfilled your duty. *Then* you may go home.

*(**ARCHER** hands him the phone.)*

(of phone) Who the fuck is it?

*(**ARCHER** hands him a card.)*

ARCHER. Your Indian…

CHARLES. Dwight? Dwight…?

(of card)

ARCHER. *(looks)* "Grackle…?" "Chief Dwight Grackle."

CHARLES. *(to phone)* Chief Grackle. Yaas, that's right, this is who that is…waal, Dwight, it's an honor to talk to you, too…

(pause) Yes, that was a fine day.

(pause) How is…

(is pointed out card) Tish?

(pause) She *did*…When? I am so sorry…

(to **ARCHER***)* Whoever last revised these cards, she's fired.

(to phone) Yes, yes, no, I remember *meeting* her at the… uh…I'm so sorry, Dwight. *So* sorry.

(pause) How…Hunting a *what?*

(pause) Well, these things happen.

(pause)

(to **ARCHER***)* It's got to be on the *card,* people.

(to phone) …Dwight: I am calling…no, no, you get the kettle…you get that teakettle!!

(to **ARCHER***)* His wife died hunting a fuckin walrus, and it's not on the card…She was eaten by a walrus…

(pause; to phone) Dwight? Dwight. You got yer tea? You all set? Dwight: I am calling you in your tribal capacity…and tis an honor to communicate with *you.*

(pause; covers phone) "The heads of two great nations"… *(shakes his head; to self)* Fucken, I don't know. I just don't know anymore.

(to phone) Dwight: well, no, it's not about the Hotel-Casino, Dw…Of *course.* I would be *more* than glad to… no, *you* go first.

(pause) Uh huh…uh huh.

(pause) Four…hundred beds…four *thousand* beds On the so-called National Seashore Preserve on Nantucket. Whew. Dwight, what do you mean "so-called…"

(to **ARCHER***)* Because the Treaty of Porcupine Cove ensured to the Micmac Nation….

(to phone) …sovereign rights in perpetuity…uh huh… Yaas, yaas, Dwight. Yas. We have to go into that…I'm sorry, I thought you'd finished.

*(***BERNSTEIN*** sneezes.)*

CHARLES. *(cont.)* Gesundheit.

> *(He motions for her to sit; to phone.)* Dwight, I need a small favor. I'd like you to announce that, as may be the case, you have discovered that the original Thanksgiving was celebrated not with "turkey," but with codfish. Which your, of course, people knew as tuna.

> *(pause)* God bless you, Dwight, now, tell me how I can express my gratitude.

> *(pause)* Well, then, I wasn't listening.

> *(pause)* Ha, ha, no, but seriously...

> *(pause)* That's...Dwight, well, yeah, fine I understand you said the *words* "that's the deal." But I hardly...Just to say the fucken codfish was a *tuna*...? You're out of your...I can't, by executive fiat give you Nantucket Island. Well, I can't give you half of Nantucket Island.

ARCHER. ...It's the National Wildlife Refuge.

CHARLES. It's the National Wildlife Refuge....

> *(listens)* "Under the terms of Porcupine Cove"...

> *(pause)* Well, maybe so, but I'm not at all sure *that* I want to give you half of...

> *(BERNSTEIN starts to leave.)*

> *(to BERNSTEIN)* Sit the fuck down.

> *(to phone)* Fuck the Treaty of Porcupine Cove, D... Dwight.

> *(pause)* What, are you nuts?

> *(pause)* I'M CALLING YOU TO ASK A *FAVOR.* DWIGHT? NO, THIS, NO. YOUR "RESPONSE" IS HARDLY IN THE NATURE OF A... A "favor" is, I'll tell you what a favor is: to pick my kids up after soccer. *That's* a favor. To give you the federal Nature Preserve on Nantucket to build a four thousand bed casino... That is not a favor, Dwight.

> *(BERNSTEIN lies down on the couch.)*

> That is highway rrr...yes, I am aware that "I called you," Dwight, you know, it might be in, a thinking man, in your best interest to have, in your "pouch" a

CHARLES. *(cont.)* favor owed you by the President of the... No, Dwight, I intended nothing by the use of the word "pouch." Dd...Dwight, no, it is not a word I do associate with Native Americans...it is...Dwight, people have...

ARCHER. Tobacco pouches.

CHARLES. Tobacco pouches, uh uh...DW...kanga-fuckin-roos have pouches.

ARCHER. Opossums.

CHARLES. Dwight. Opossums have pouches. I intended nothing by my use of...well, well, fuck you, too. Fucken dime store Indian...Yes, yes, I said it, and...

(to **ARCHER***)* He's taping the call.

(to phone) I don't give a fuck if you're taping reruns of Bonanza. Well, why don't you fucken ride *down* here, Dwight, and *extract* revenge. Why'nt you do that...? On your no doubt Painted Pony. Hey, I'll leave a pass at the gate...

(to **ARCHER***)* Leave a pass at the gate for Chief DWIGHT GRACKLE of the Micmac Nation.

(to phone) Yes, yes, Dwight, I *did* use that term disparagingly...

(to **ARCHER***)* ...a "hate crime"...

(to phone) Oh, really, well, well, Dwight. *I CAN'T SAY I CARE.* You know why? Because I can't be *convicted* of crimes.

I can resign tomorrow and my Vice President...

(to **ARCHER***)* What's his name?

*(***ARCHER** *shrugs.)*

Will pardon me for crimes yet uninvented. Yes, while *you,* "Tonto," are on a plane to nowhere. And I hope your second wife gets eaten by a walrus...

(listens; to **ARCHER***)* In Micmac, that's apparently the worst thing you can say... He's going to send his braves down to extract revenge.

(to phone) Well, Dwight, how'd you like a ride? I'll tell the Secret Service to come by and put you on the

piggyplane to Prybschych *fuckin* Bulgaria with a price-less view of the Bumfuck Mountains, 'cept you will not see them, being encased in sixteen cubic feet of con-crete, 'til the flesh molts on your body and falls in a tidy pile around your fucking, *fucking,* "terrorist" ass. Now *you* talk:

(pause) Well, fuck you, too.

(CHARLES hangs up.)

(The phone rings. ARCHER answers.)

ARCHER. *(to phone)* Yes...

(hangs up; to CHARLES) The Turkey guys. One-ninety-five, is as high as they'll go.

(pause)

CHARLES. Yeah, you're the ruler of the free world, every-one's your friend. You're not, you're just another "working stiff."

(pause) Who can we shake down...?

ARCHER. Chucky...It's over.

CHARLES. No. Arch, I'd have to go home broke.

ARCHER. Take the one-ninety-five.

CHARLES. No Library...

ARCHER. Not everybody gets a Library.

CHARLES. Someday. Some "researcher", In some deep *repos-itory* of our nation's papers. Some budding "historian," devoted to "the life of the mind," will come across a note. That, in the past, there was such a figure, as CHARLES H.P. Smith. That he lived, and suffered. Who was he?

ARCHER. Who?

CHARLES. He was "a man."

(pause) No, Archer. No. I have built no bridges, cured no disease; and the great problems which I found, I leave behind me. Did I understand "the world?" Who does? I went from day to day, trying to stumble forward

CHARLES. *(cont.)* by the light of those poor gifts I had. But somewhere, perhaps, in "the mind of God," I'll be judged not by my "self-assessment," but by the needs of the Great Hidden Scheme. And I'll be found to have served my purpose.

(pause)

What is immortality?

ARCHER. It is the ability to live forever.

CHARLES. Indeed it is. But *my* legacy. Will die on Tuesday, when that wanker gets elected.

ARCHER. I know. It's wrong.

CHARLES. A harsh world, Bernstein, is it not...?

BERNSTEIN. *(waking up)* Sir...

CHARLES. Harsh world. Especially for *you.*

BERNSTEIN. For me?

CHARLES. As you are a lesbian.

BERNSTEIN. In essence, yes.

CHARLES. Thus, your day, must abound with constant horrendous disappointments, insults and betrayals.

BERNSTEIN. I endeavor, Sir, to live my life with self-respect.

CHARLES. That's laudable, Bernstein. It's more than laudable, it's saintly.

BERNSTEIN. Thank you, Sir.

CHARLES. In spite of your loathsome, and abominable practices. For, Bernstein, you have been a good friend to me.

BERNSTEIN. Thank you, Sir.

CHARLES. A good friend to a failure. Yes. A man, who looks back. On his life. What does he see? But missteps, squandered opportunities, betrayal...loss.

BERNSTEIN. I'm sorry for your troubles, Sir.

(She sneezes.)

CHARLES. ...to this man...gesundheit,

BERNSTEIN. Thank you.

CHARLES. ...everything is wrong. *(BERNSTEIN sneezes again)* Go home. The Good and the Bad:

BERNSTEIN. I'll come in tomorrow, Sir, with your concession speech.

CHARLES. ...all wrong.

BERNSTEIN. *(gathering up her things)* God bless you, Sir.

CHARLES. Restraint and effort...

ARCHER. ...mmm, hmm...

CHARLES. Right and Left. War and Peace.

BERNSTEIN. Bye-bye.

CHARLES. Sin and Redemption... All wrong.

ARCHER. Point to one thing which is not wrong.

   (pause)

BERNSTEIN. I'll see you tomorrow, Sir.

CHARLES. Hold on: what if *Thanksgiving* is wrong?

ARCHER. I don't get it.

CHARLES. Thanksgiving is wrong.

ARCHER. Why?

CHARLES. *Bernstein:*

BERNSTEIN. *(at the door)* Sir.

CHARLES. Thanksgiving is wrong.

BERNSTEIN. I don't understand.

CHARLES. We, we had "slavery" for years.

BERNSTEIN. Yes.

CHARLES. That was wrong...We had, I'm sure there are other instances...uh, "disco"...things that we did in our ignorance, Bernstein. But, what makes this country great?

BERNSTEIN. Sir?

CHARLES. We Have the Power to Correct Ourselves...

BERNSTEIN. "Thanksgiving is wrong..."

CHARLES. Off the top of your head.

BERNSTEIN. *Thanksgiving.*

CHARLES. Yes.

BERNSTEIN. Is a Eurocentric holiday, uh, which...

CHARLES. Wrongs, Bernstein…

BERNSTEIN. …Yes…?

CHARLES. Have *victims.*

BERNSTEIN. Sir, that is true –

CHARLES. Who are the victims of Thanksgiving, Bernstein?

BERNSTEIN. …are they the turkeys, Sir?

CHARLES. They are the turkeys. Write me that speech. Archer:

ARCHER. Sir?

CHARLES. Do I have the power to pardon turkeys?

ARCHER. Mister President, you do.

CHARLES. Tell them I want two hundred million dollars in cash, on my desk by breakfast, or I'm going to pardon *Every Fucken Turkey In This Country.*

End of Act I

ACT TWO

(The men in shirtsleeves. **BERNSTEIN** *at a typewriter –*
typing paper all around her.)

ARCHER. We can't build the fence to keep out the illegal
immigrants.

CHARLES. Why not?

ARCHER. You need the illegal immigrants to build the
fence.

CHARLES. It's always something.

ARCHER. And you can't pardon all the turkeys.

CHARLES. I can pardon whoever I like. Clinton proved that.

ARCHER. That is, you can "pardon" all the turkeys but, the
people will still eat them.

CHARLES. Not after Bernstein's speech.

BERNSTEIN. When I've finished my speech, may I go home?

CHARLES. Why is Thanksgiving wrong?

BERNSTEIN. Because it celebrates…

CHARLES. Yes:

BERNSTEIN. Patriarchy.

CHARLES. Okay.

BERNSTEIN. Exploitation of indigenous…

CHARLES. …I'm listening.

BERNSTEIN. …peoples and conspicuous consumption.

CHARLES. Uh huh…

BERNSTEIN. Combined under the auspices of a seemingly
non-governmental holiday which is, in essence, a
hymn to the power of the state.

(pause)

CHARLES. Yeah, you have to start again.

BERNSTEIN. Why?

CHARLES. Lookit:

> *(pause)* You want to rile people up, you've got to give them something to like better than the things they like, OR something to HATE better than the things they like...You can tell them a good IDEA, but, that only works, if it lets them DO something, which, they couldn't, course of events, do. Like Free Love or something.
>
> *(pause)* That's what we're aiming for. Throw in some sex for God's sake.

BERNSTEIN. Oh.

> *(pause)* Alright: Thanksgiving was not, originally, a holiday of thanks, or harvest, but a historic day of orgy. When the Native Americans cast off all shackles of...

CHARLES. ...Uh huh.

BERNSTEIN. Sexual restraint.

CHARLES. Well, now you're talking.

BERNSTEIN. And cavorted, naked...

CHARLES. ...I love it already...

BERNSTEIN. ...while the blessed feast cooled on the table.

> *(pause)* Now may I go home...?

CHARLES. So all this bullshit about the Indians and turkeys was, in essence, code for the, uh, race-mixing...

BERNSTEIN. ...yes

CHARLES. ...polysexual abandon which...

BERNSTEIN. Sure...

CHARLES. The quote quote Pilgrims...

BERNSTEIN. *(sneezes)* I need to go home, sir.

CHARLES. Yeah, yeah, you're going home.

BERNSTEIN. I need to see my baby.

CHARLES. Almost there...proved by a set of documents, discovered JUST THIS MORNING by Navy Seals, diving off of Plymouth Rock, in the wreck of a 1642, uh uh...

ARCHER. ...excursion boat.

CHARLES. In the handwriting of a nondenominational minister...

ARCHER. Good.

CHARLES. ...in which he CONFESSES, that Thanksgiving was a day of orgy, and that those who celebrate it are damned...screw with me, will ya...? Bring in the turkey guy.

(The **TURKEY GUY** *enters.)*

TURKEY GUY. Mr. President.

CHARLES. Yeah, hi.

TURKEY GUY. Sir, I regret my intemperate and disrespectful words...

CHARLES. These things happen.

TURKEY GUY. And I would like to raise my offer to three hundred thousand dollars.

CHARLES. You remember my speechwriter?

TURKEY GUY. ...along with my *profound* apology.

CHARLES. Hey, you called me one, I called you one.

TURKEY GUY. Most gracious, Sir.

CHARLES. Hey, look.

(They shake hands.)

TURKEY GUY. The turkeys need to smell your hand. And then I must return them to their climate-controlled transport.

CHARLES. That's what YOU want, what do *I* want?

TURKEY GUY. Social justice?

CHARLES. That would be swell, but what I, in my heart desire is two hundred million dollars.
(pause) Or I'm going on TV and pardon all the turkeys in the world.

TURKEY GUY. I...

CHARLES. You know why? Thanksgiving is wrong. Hit it.

BERNSTEIN. It's a confected celebration of the evils of oppression...

TURKEY GUY. I...

CHARLES. Yep, Thanksgiving is wrong.

TURKEY GUY. The American people will never *never* buy it.

CHARLES. You hear the speech, then *you* tell me...Now hit the bricks, and bring me something green and wrinkled.

(*The* **TURKEY GUY** *exits.*)

ARCHER. But will the American people actually give up Thanksgiving?

CHARLES. Bernstein?

BERNSTEIN. Things change.

(**BERNSTEIN** *hands him a piece of the speech and keeps typing.*)

CHARLES. (*reads*) "Our ideas change. Things change. Time passes. We age, and see things, in a new light, a low winter light, which points the way toward spring." Yeah...you're what I love about this country.

BERNSTEIN. I am sir?

CHARLES. You bet. I know what you would like, is to take over the government of the United States by force, promoting your vision of a godless, stateless paradise of homosexuality...is that correct...?

BERNSTEIN. Essentially.

CHARLES. But you know what you have?

BERNSTEIN. Sir?

CHARLES. A work ethic.

BERNSTEIN. Thank you, Sir.

CHARLES. You roll your sleeves up and muck *in.*

BERNSTEIN. Thank you.

CHARLES. You're not some frikkin "expert."

BERNSTEIN. No, Sir.

CHARLES. The experts cost me this election. They didn't build this country.

BERNSTEIN. No.

CHARLES. Who built this country?

BERNSTEIN. Sir?

CHARLES. Shade tree mechanics. Tom Edison. Henry Ford.

BERNSTEIN. Are they sending a car to take me home…?

CHARLES. They're trine 'a rent you one. The Wright Brothers…*Tinkerers*…couple guys, sitting round the Coffee Corner, Wednesday morning…

(BERNSTEIN sneezes.

(CHARLES hands her a Kleenex.)

Some fella, doodlin on a *napkin*…Dreaming. He looks up: "Hey. I betcha *this'll* work…"

(BERNSTEIN sneezes.)

Uh, Jonas Salk gets up one day, "Hey, you know what? *Fuck* polio…" "Experts?" What's an expert? That's not who made this country great. Who made this country great?

ARCHER. Who?

CHARLES. Shade tree mechanics. Just like you. Just like *me*. Huh?

BERNSTEIN. "Shade tree mechanics."

CHARLES. That's right. People with a vision.

BERNSTEIN. "Just like you and me…"

CHARLES. …that's right…

BERNSTEIN. The people at the water cooler…

CHARLES. Yes…

BERNSTEIN. We don't know their politics…

CHARLES. …no…

BERNSTEIN. N' we wouldn't think to ask them.

CHARLES. …that's right.

BERNSTEIN. …for we respect their right to be different.

CHARLES. Yeah, yeah, I get it. It's true, though. Isn't it…?

BERNSTEIN. Yes, Sir. It's true. And it's what people need to hear.

CHARLES. *(reading)* A low light…a low winter light.

CHARLES. *(cont.)* "Which points the way toward spring…"
And toward two hundred million dollars. To stick in
my fucking pocket.

(pause) You've stopped writing, Bernstein.

BERNSTEIN. That's right.

CHARLES. Could you tell me why?

BERNSTEIN. I feel, Sir, on reflection, perhaps this speech
falls outside the purview of my duties as enumerated.

CHARLES. Say it again.

BERNSTEIN. It occurs to me you want me to indulge in an
exercise in extortion.

CHARLES. That's right. And I'll tell you what: I'll give you in
return – whatever you want. I'm like the Chinese. You
want something from the Chinese, you go over there
and *trade* them for it.

BERNSTEIN. I don't understand.

CHARLES. You paid, if I'm not out of court, twenty-five
grand for your baby.

BERNSTEIN. I did not pay, sir, for the baby, which would be
trafficking in human flesh.

CHARLES. What did you pay for?

BERNSTEIN. How do you know I paid?

CHARLES. You paid twenty-five grand from the *credit card.*

BERNSTEIN. You investigated my credit card account?

CHARLES. Oh, grow up.

BERNSTEIN. I *paid,* sir…

CHARLES. …*ooo*kay.

BERNSTEIN. Administrative costs, associated with…

CHARLES. Yeah, okay. I get it. I get it.

BERNSTEIN. I insist that you amend your language.

CHARLES. Uh huh.

BERNSTEIN. I insist on that point.

CHARLES. To *who? Get* it? Ain't *nobody* in this room but us.
All your fricken bullshit about "social justice". That's
swell. What you *forgot:* THIS IS A DEMOCRACY. Which

means: The *people* make the laws. And if *you* want to make the laws, you *go* to the people who make the laws, and what do you do?

ARCHER. You bribe them.

CHARLES. YOU BRIBE THEM. You give them something *they'd* like. In order to get something *you'd* like. Just like you did in third grade.

ARCHER. That's right.

CHARLES. You say, "Gimme your candy bar and I'll give you my orange."

BERNSTEIN. I...

CHARLES. You do *not* say: Give me your candy bar, because it exploits the cocoa workers in Brazil...

ARCHER. *Chucky.*

CHARLES. Because I heard it on Public Radio.

ARCHER. Chuck.

CHARLES. I could couch my language in the fucken gibberism you speak. But I'm addressing you, like I'd talk to anyone else, because, you say *that* in the schoolyard, and the other kid says "fuck you." Weep weep weep you say, I'll take this case to the Supreme Court. Guess what: the Supreme *Court* wants something, too. Everyone wants something. The power. To trade this for that separates us from the lower life forms, like the uh uh large apes, or the Scandinavians. I *like* you, Bernstein. You know why? You're great at what you do. Do I respect you? Fuck no. Why? Your head is full of trash. But you can sling the shit. I'll pay you for that. I will pay you for that speech – What do you want? *(pause)*

BERNSTEIN. I want to marry my partner.

CHARLES. I can't do that.

BERNSTEIN. Yes, you can.

CHARLES. It's against the law.

BERNSTEIN. Figure it out.

CHARLES. Write me my speech.

BERNSTEIN. You figure it out, I'll write your speech.

CHARLES. Goddamnit, Bernstein, I want that speech.

(She hands him a speech.)

"My fellow Americans, it is with a real regret, that I bid you and this office adieu." This is my *concession* speech.

BERNSTEIN. That's right.

CHARLES. Ha ha ha, I want the *other* speech.

BERNSTEIN. I told you my terms.

CHARLES. I cannot do what you ask. It's illegal.

BERNSTEIN. There is a higher law.

CHARLES. Oh, *bullshit.*

BERNSTEIN. There is a higher law.

CHARLES. What's it called, if you're so smart.

BERNSTEIN. It is the law of love.

CHARLES. Oh, that's a law? Where is *that* law written? On your Chinese *amulet*?

(He picks up her amulet.)

All *you* know, this says "don't starch the sheets".

BERNSTEIN. Mr. President.

CHARLES. I cannot marry you to a girl. It. Is. Illegal.

BERNSTEIN. Did you ever have a homosexual experience?

CHARLES. I'm not telling.

(pause)

BERNSTEIN. *(exiting)* Well, you know my terms.

CHARLES. You walk out that door, I'm sending you to Prybschych, Bulgaria.

BERNSTEIN. You wouldn't dare.

CHARLES. Try me.

BERNSTEIN. *That's* breaking the law.

CHARLES. NOT IF I DON'T GET CAUGHT.

BERNSTEIN. How is that not breaking the law? To torture people.

CHARLES. I'm not here to play "word games"…

ARCHER. Sometimes.

BERNSTEIN. …yes.

ARCHER. "Bernstein."

BERNSTEIN. Yes…

ARCHER. The "state"…You recognize the right to existence of The State…

BERNSTEIN. …not when it acts unjustly.

ARCHER. Must take actions *which*, though not…

CHARLES. Yes.

ARCHER. Clearly *authorized* by law. Must, in the service of a *higher* law…

BERNSTEIN. …that's what I'm telling you.

CHARLES. Okay, okay, alright, tell you what: I'll "marry" you and your partner, what is her name?

BERNSTEIN. I don't want any jokes.

CHARLES. All right.

BERNSTEIN. My partner's name is Daisy.

CHARLES. All right. That's all right with me.

BERNSTEIN. It's her name *irrespective* of whether or not it's all right with…

CHARLES. I SAID ALL-FUCKEN-*RIGHT*, OKAY? WHAT ARE YOU, BITCH BITCH BITCH, I'M TRINE…

BERNSTEIN. Please lower your voice.

CHARLES. I'm sorry.

BERNSTEIN. And I'd like to go home to my baby.

CHARLES. As soon as you write my speech.

BERNSTEIN. Give me your word you'll marry us.

CHARLES. Jesus Christ, you broads got a one track mind.

BERNSTEIN. After the revolution, comments like that will get you taken out and shot.

CHARLES. Well, give me some warning, so I can look my best.

BERNSTEIN. Fuck you.

CHARLES. Cause, I'd hate for em to drag me out and *shoot* me, with my *hair* mussed…

BERNSTEIN. Fuck you.

CHARLES. ...or full of straw from sleeping on a fucken *Tumbrel*...

BERNSTEIN. Fuck you.

CHARLES. And fuck *you,* too. You, fucken, *SPEECH WRITER.* FUCK *YOU.*

BERNSTEIN. ...if I were a man.

CHARLES. IF YOU WERE A MAN, I'D OF HAD YOU BEAT TO DEATH WITH A ROCK. *DON'T YOU GET IT*? ALL THIS BUSHWA "OPPRESSION" YOU'RE BITCHING ABOUT, IS ON A FREE *PASS.* A. FREE. PASS. CAUSE YOU'RE A *BROAD.* What the hell...I don't care. Ship her to...

ARCHER. ...don't say it.

CHARLES. ...put her on the piggyplane and ship her to Bulgaria, I'm done. Where are the Secret Service?

ARCHER. Sensitivity training. *(pause)* It's non-optional.

CHARLES. Get 'em and drag her out of here.

(ARCHER exits.)

BERNSTEIN. What is my crime?

CHARLES. You get on my ass. It's not *worth* being President. *Fuck* it. Tell the turkey people keep their money. I concede.

Don't worry about *me.* Don't worry about *my* wife. We count for nothing. We're not human. We're not homosexual. Or black. Or Palestinian, or *deaf,* or something. All we are is *normal.* Fucken normal guy... hey, the hell with it. Gimme the concession speech...

(pause)

BERNSTEIN. Mr. President.

CHARLES. ...Fucken "what"...?

BERNSTEIN. I think you are human.

CHARLES. ...thank you.

BERNSTEIN. And, I realize, you are perhaps under a bit of pressure.

CHARLES. Oh, do you think so?

BERNSTEIN. And that your "time in office" is waning.

CHARLES. Well, Bernstein, quack quack, you know what I mean?

BERNSTEIN. Sir, I do. And I would like to *ask* you...

CHARLES. Yes.

BERNSTEIN. In the interest of humanity.

CHARLES. Yes.

BERNSTEIN. *In* this waning time.

CHARLES. All right.

BERNSTEIN. To do something pure.

(pause)

CHARLES. And what is that that is pure?

BERNSTEIN. To marry. Two people who love each other.

(pause)

CHARLES. It's not legal.

BERNSTEIN. You could *make* it legal.

CHARLES. At what cost, Bernstein? Riots? Backlash? *We* don't know...

BERNSTEIN. Sir?

CHARLES. *(cont.)* We don't know. This is the way the world *works.* There *are* no solutions, Bernstein. There are only rearrangements of problems.

(pause) New ways of looking at problems.

BERNSTEIN. Isn't that what we do best, sir?

CHARLES. What're we talking about?

BERNSTEIN. This "nation of tinkerers."

(pause) Isn't that America?

CHARLES. I...

BERNSTEIN. The fellow or the woman at the water cooler? *We* don't know their politics. We judge their character by the simple things: Are they respectful, are they *punctual,* can they *listen,* "can they get along"... We care if they paint their fence. *We* don't know who they vote for.

CHARLES. ...no...

BERNSTEIN. We don't know "what they do in *bed...*" Who would be disrespectful enough to inquire...?

CHARLES. ...yes...

BERNSTEIN. If you look at the *polls...*

(*sneezes*)

CHARLES. Gesundheit.

BERNSTEIN. It seems: We are "a nation divided." But: *We* aren't a "nation divided," Sir. We're a democracy – we hold different opinions. But: We laugh at the same jokes, we clap each other on the back, when we made that month's *quota*, and, sir, I'm not at all sure that we don't love each other.

(*pause*)

CHARLES. This is a great speech, Bernstein.

BERNSTEIN. Let's talk about hard times. Fellow, woman, loses their job. Middle age, the world turns upside down. "What did I do 'wrong?"

CHARLES. ...that's true...

BERNSTEIN. ...you reach a certain age, and you've *been* there. Perhaps you're there *now...*

CHARLES. ...I *am* there now.

BERNSTEIN. ...and you have suffered a *reversal.* What does it bring?

CHARLES. ...I give.

BERNSTEIN. It brings *strength...*

(*pause*)

CHARLES. It does?

BERNSTEIN. It does. It brings *humility...*

(**ARCHER** *re-enters.*)

And it brings wisdom.

(*pause*)

ARCHER. They blinked.

BERNSTEIN. And that is the position, sir, in which we find you now.

ARCHER. ...Chucky.

(*pause*)

CHARLES. (*to* BERNSTEIN) ...I don't understand.

BERNSTEIN. A man. At a difficult time. Finds himself. Faced with hard choices. As the leader. Of a group. Of Shade Tree Mechanics. (*pause*) Of workers.

ARCHER. Mister President...?

BERNSTEIN. Which, as a convenience, we refer to as "The United States of America."

(*pause*)

ARCHER. Mister President.

(*pause*)

ARCHER. Chucky...

CHARLES. What?

ARCHER. The turkey folks. Will go two hundred million dollars.

(*pause*) They'll go the two hundred million bucks. You're going home rich.

CHARLES. Archer.

ARCHER. ...Sir.

CHARLES. Call the networks. Tell them we're buying two hundred million dollars worth of airtime. Bernstein, you go finish that speech. I'll be goddamned if I'm not going to win this thing.

End of Act II

ACT III

(The Office, morning.)

(The President is changing his shirt and shaving.)

CHARLES. *(to phone)* Barry. Yes. I'm surprised you still have my number.

(pause) Yaas. You heard that? Waal, we have quote, set aside a little money for a little airtime.

(pause)

(ARCHER *enters with a tray, bearing coffee and so on.)*

Oh, two hundred million dollars. Waal, Barry, we've got an "election" coming up, and, waal, we sort of, thought we'd like to "win" it.

(pause) We got it from some "people" you know...

ARCHER. ...What does he want...?

CHARLES. *(covering phone)* He heard we made a little "airbuy."

(to phone) Yes. It *is* a lot of money to spend in ONE WEEK, IN THE LAST WEEK, BARRY, BEFORE THAT ELECTION IN WHICH YOU AND THE COMMITTEE KICKED ME TO THE CURB.

(to **ARCHER***)* "Why didn't we check with him?"

*(***CHARLES** *hands the phone to* **ARCHER***.)*

ARCHER. *(to phone)* Waal, Barry, we didn't check with you cause you told us to "go fuck" ourselves...

CHARLES. Tell *him* to go and fuck himself.

ARCHER. Barry...

CHARLES. *(seizing the phone)* Gimme that phone.... *(to phone)* No, Barry, we did *not* "take your remarks out of context," so, let's skip the lovemaking, and what do you want?

CHARLES. *(cont.)* *(to* **ARCHER***)* He wants to "get on board"

    (pause)

Well, Barry, you have me at a disadvantage because I don't *give* a fuck.

(to **ARCHER***)* He's found some money…

(to phone) Where did the money come from, Barry? Cause, yesterday you were *broke?* Did you forget to look in the GLOVE COMPARTMENT? Barry? Did you forget to look behind the couch? Cause "behind the couch" that's where *I* always look, when *I* need to find two hundred million dollars, to help out my friend, to who you swore undying brotherhood, and then turned around and cut him off at the ankles with ONE SPOT IN CINCINNATI and his wife had to CRY HERSELF TO SLEEP because you wouldn't even have the courtesy to buy him a LIBRARY, after everything he did for you. *D'YOU LOOK BEHIND THE COUCH?* What? No – you're right, you're right, Barr – yesterday was yesterday, today's today, and we go on.

(pause) You're right – we have to work together. No – you're right – not at all. Not at all. Barr – on we go.

(Hangs up phone.)

(to **ARCHER***)* Call the I.R.S. and have him audited back to the day he was born. *(pause)* And get someone to kill his cat.

(Pause. The phone rings. **ARCHER** *answers.)*

ARCHER. *(To phone)* Send him in.

    *(*TURKEY GUY *enters.)*

TURKEY GUY. Mr. President.

CHARLES. Yes.

TURKEY GUY. I had to move the turkeys from their climate-controlled capsule.

CHARLES. Where are they now?

TURKEY GUY. They're in the outer office.

CHARLES. That's lovely.

TURKEY GUY. And they need to smell your hand.

CHARLES. Alright.

TURKEY GUY. And, Sir, there are people coughing in the anteroom.

ARCHER. *(to phone)* Tell the people in the anteroom to stop coughing.

TURKEY GUY. And we would like to see the speech.

ARCHER. You need to see the speech?

TURKEY GUY. Yes.

ARCHER. *We* need to see the money.

TURKEY GUY. And I need you to permit the turkeys to smell your hand.

ARCHER. He wants the turkeys to smell your hand.

CHARLES. Yeah, back up and repeat the bit about the "money."

ARCHER. You get the money *after* you pardon the turkeys.

CHARLES. What's to prevent him from reneging? I pardon his turkeys, and he says, "Thanks a lot, lame duck. See you in the funny papers." What then?

ARCHER. You put him on the piggy plane.

CHARLES. *(to the* **TURKEY GUY***)* You get the idea?

TURKEY GUY. I am so looking forward to working with you sir.

CHARLES. After the broadcast, you give me the money.

TURKEY GUY. That is correct.

CHARLES. And, I am looking forward to working with you too, pal. Four more wondrous years.

TURKEY GUY. Four more years of …?

CHARLES. Of my presidency.

*(***BERNSTEIN*** shows up, sneezing, in a wedding dress, her amulet around her neck.)*

BERNSTEIN. Sir, good morning. Achoo.

CHARLES. You sick?

BERNSTEIN. Just something I caught on the plane…

(Sneezes)

CHARLES. Get someone from Walter Reed down here with some penicillin.

ARCHER. *(to phone)* Gemma a doctor with some penicillin.

BERNSTEIN. Sir, on behalf of my partner, our daughter, *and* myself.

ARCHER. Is that a wedding dress?

BERNSTEIN. Sir, it is.

ARCHER. It's lovely.

BERNSTEIN. Thank you, sir.

>   *(hands him speech)* I think you'll like this...

ARCHER. Why are you wearing it?

CHARLES. *(of speech)* Oh, jeez, listen to this:

>   *(All sit. The phone rings.)*

ARCHER. *(to phone)* Yes. The TV people want to do a sound check.

CHARLES. Coming right down.

TURKEY GUY. Please tell them to place the turkeys on stage, so that they become accustomed to the noise and the commotion.

ARCHER. Sure.

TURKEY GUY. But not too near the lights.

ARCHER. *(To phone.)* Put the turkeys in the studio.

>   *(hangs up)*

BERNSTEIN. *(reads)* "A country. Like a family, like a race, or a religion, like a *business*..."

CHARLES. Business, good.

BERNSTEIN. "...is an organic enterprise. Because it *lives*, it *changes*..."

TURKEY GUY. ...Sir, might I hear the part about the turkeys...

BERNSTEIN. "...it has its triumphs, and, of course, it makes mistakes, in short, it *grows*. Now: we've all heard the phrase 'growing pains...'"

>   *(The phone rings.)*

ARCHER. *(LISTENS, THEN to* **TURKEY GUY***)* They want you out there.

TURKEY GUY. Excuse me...

(**TURKEY GUY** *exits.*)

CHARLES. Bernstein, this *speech?* This *here...?*

BERNSTEIN. Thank you, sir.

CHARLES. This makes me sound smart.

ARCHER. Why are you wearing a wedding dress?

BERNSTEIN. *(to* **CHARLES***)* ...thank you.

CHARLES. *Thank* me? Thank *you...* What do *you* want? You tell me: Ambassador to what, France? Somewhere closer?

BERNSTEIN. Sir.

CHARLES. You name it: the U.N. ...are we still in the U.N.?

ARCHER. You want me to check?

BERNSTEIN. Sir, all I and my *partner,* and our *daughter* want. Is the *one thing.* And for you to, in your second term, to be well, do good, live *long,* and deal justly.

(*pause*)

CHARLES. I love this speech Bernstein. I love it and I will do everything in my power to do ALL those things.

ARCHER. A-plus speech, Bernstein.

BERNSTEIN. Wait til it's done...!

ARCHER. ...and why are you wearing a wedding dress?

BERNSTEIN. I'm getting married.

CHARLES. No, I believe he means why are you wearing a wedding dress *today?*

BERNSTEIN. I'm getting *married* today.

ARCHER. ...and there's *another* woman in a wedding dress.

BERNSTEIN. Yes.

ARCHER. In the outer office...

BERNSTEIN. That would be my partner.

ARCHER. *Uh* huh...

BERNSTEIN. And, sir.

CHARLES. Yes.

BERNSTEIN. I have the one more favor…

CHARLES. You ask it, pal.

BERNSTEIN. My partner and I…would be *honored,* if you'd let us name our daughter after you.

CHARLES. Bernstein, can I give you a "hug"?

BERNSTEIN. If you're not reluctant, Sir, to "hug" a person of a differing sexual orientation.

CHARLES. I've been doing it all my life.

(**CHARLES** *and* **BERNSTEIN** *hug.*)

BERNSTEIN. Thank you, sir.

CHARLES. That speech, Bernstein, is my legacy.

BERNSTEIN. You wait til it's *done.*

CHARLES. It's not done?

BERNSTEIN. It's almost done…

CHARLES. Can I see it now?

BERNSTEIN. Not til it's done.

CHARLES. When will it *be* done.

BERNSTEIN. After we're married.

CHARLES. But I need it now to do it on T.V.

BERNSTEIN. We thought, you'd marry us on T.V. *first,* and, *then,* I'd give you your speech.

(*pause*)

CHARLES. Don't you *trust* me, Bernstein?

BERNSTEIN. Sir? I don't trust *anyone.* But, if I did? I'd trust you first.

CHARLES. Bernstein, I am the president.

BERNSTEIN. That's what I'm saying, sir.

CHARLES. I don't get the speech, until I marry you on T.V.

BERNSTEIN. That is correct. I am so excited.

(**BERNSTEIN** *exits.*)

CHARLES. Find out how I can marry the broad…

ARCHER. You can't do that.

CHARLES. I need that speech.

ARCHER. It's illegal.

CHARLES. Make it legal.

ARCHER. I can't do that.

CHARLES. Then why are you my *lawyer?*

ARCHER. I can't do anything "illegal."

CHARLES. What we're speaking of, would be illegal?

ARCHER. It would be illegal.

CHARLES. Thus, it would be a "crime."

ARCHER. Yes.

CHARLES. And, thus "against the law."

ARCHER. That is the nature of a crime.

CHARLES. How twisted are the works of man.

(*pause*) Find some way to make it legal.

ARCHER. It's legal in Massachusetts.

CHARLES. Is that the way you want to live your life?

ARCHER. ..it'll cause precedent.

CHARLES. Not necessarily.

ARCHER. That's what LEGAL *is.*

CHARLES. It is?

ARCHER. "LEGAL" means making a precedent, so that, NEXT time in the same circumstances, people know what to do.

(*pause*) Because they know what's legal.

(*pause*) That's what it means, "a legal precedent."

(*pause*)

CHARLES. What about a, okay, okay, what about a "bill," for just one person.

ARCHER. ...that's illegal.

CHARLES. ...it's "ill" – egal. Can't I do it under "executive powers"?

ARCHER. Legally, no.

CHARLES. What about "illegally"?

ARCHER. It wouldn't be legal.

CHARLES. Okay. What about if it, okay: WASN'T "legal,"

but, BUT, it "looked" legal for *just enough time*, before
the Supreme Court tromped in and said it was, what
do they say...? "Nonconstitutional."

CHARLES. *(cont.)* *(pause)* That's all I need. Let them "de
legalize" it next week. Isn't that what they *do*? *I* don't
give a fuck...

ARCHER. ...they'd say you quote quote "seized the reins of
power."

CHARLES. What would I do with "the reins of power?" I just
wanna get re-elected.

ARCHER. ...it has to be legal.

CHARLES. Fucken *legal.*
    (pause) What *is* legal? Is it "legal" for the State to deny
    of two perfectly good citizens, the right to "get mar-
    ried," just because they're both girls?

ARCHER. ...yes.

CHARLES. Well, that's a crime...

ARCHER. Yeah, it's a damn shame.

CHARLES. It allows, uh uh, uh, "other" people to get mar-
    ried.

ARCHER. That it does.

CHARLES. At one time. It prohibited.

ARCHER. ...uh huh.

CHARLES. ...uh uh uh, people of other races from marry-
    ing.

ARCHER. No, it didn't.

CHARLES. It prohibited people of other races, from marry-
    ing people of other races.

ARCHER. It ain't going to fly.

CHARLES. Then help me out.

ARCHER. She insists on you "marrying" them.

CHARLES. Yes.

ARCHER. *Before* she gives you the speech?

CHARLES. Yes. *(pause)*

ARCHER. ...*women*...

CHARLES. No, they have rights, just like regular human beings.

ARCHER. As you've always said.

CHARLES. I *married* one of em.

ARCHER. You married two of em.

CHARLES. Yeah, but the first one was expunged.

(**ARCHER** *and* **CHARLES** *knock wood.*)

(**TURKEY GUY** *enters.*)

TURKEY GUY. I need you to smell the turkeys' hand.

ARCHER. Don't you say "Sir"?

TURKEY GUY. Not for two hundred million dollars.

CHARLES. (to **ARCHER**) How do I *marry* the broads?

TURKEY GUY. I need you to smell the turkeys' hand.

CHARLES. I believe you mean, you need the turkeys to smell *my* hand.

TURKEY GUY. That is correct.

CHARLES. You bet.

(*The second phone rings.* **ARCHER** *answers.*)

ARCHER. Yes...

TURKEY GUY. Because they're very sensitive.

CHARLES. Aren't we all?

ARCHER. *(to **CHARLES**)* The T.V. people. Bernstein and her pal – have refused to wear makeup.

CHARLES. That's their inalienable right. And get a license.

ARCHER. *(to phone)* Can we get a marriage license "right now"? Because he needs to marry them today.

TURKEY GUY. Who?

ARCHER. The girls in the *wedding* dress...

TURKEY GUY. He wants to marry two "women"?

ARCHER. That's right.

TURKEY GUY. Two "lesbians."

CHARLES. Well, why would two straight women get married? They marry "men."

TURKEY GUY. You, you mean to "marry two women"?

CHARLES. Oh, *I'm* sorry. *I* didn't ask your *permission.*

TURKEY GUY. *Today…?*

CHARLES. Well, I didn't say "today," but they got dressed *up* and came *down* here…

ARCHER. *(to phone)* The press wants to know why there are two women, in a wedding dress, and bouquets, sitting in the office with a little Chinese child.

CHARLES. Tell the press they all pulled each other from a burning *wreck…*

TURKEY GUY. If you marry those lesbians, we can not give you the money.

CHARLES. …or they won a *spelling* bee or something.

TURKEY GUY. If you marry those two women on T.V. We will not give you the money.

(pause)

CHARLES. That is not the spirit which made this land what it is.

TURKEY GUY. I do not *give* a fuck.

CHARLES. What is this, some anti-homosexual thing on your part?

TURKEY GUY. That may or may not be, but I speak as the representative of three hundred million God-fearing consumers of turkey.

(The phone rings. ARCHER answers.)

ARCHER. Your wife's on the line.

CHARLES. WOULD YOU TELL HER I'M *AT WORK. Jesus*, a man can *not* work at home…

TURKEY GUY. If you…

CHARLES. I HEARD YOU, alright? What *about*: hold on.

(The phone rings again. ARCHER answers.)

ARCHER. Yes…?

CHARLES. What about if I don't marry them, until *after* Thanksgiving?

ARCHER. *(to* CHARLES*)* Bernstein has explained to the press that you are marrying her at the beginning of your telecast.

TURKEY GUY. Oh my…

(pause)

ARCHER. I'll take care of it.

TURKEY GUY. My principals, will, in no circumstances allow –

ARCHER. I said I'll take care of it.

TURKEY GUY. Excuse me.

(He exits.)

ARCHER. Chuck.

CHARLES. Yes.

ARCHER. Two things you need. To win an election.

CHARLES. Yeah.

ARCHER. A shitload of money.

CHARLES. That's right.

ARCHER. AND a good idea. Here's the good idea: you have to sell Bernstein out.

CHARLES. To sell Bernstein out.

ARCHER. That's right.

CHARLES. I'm in her debt.

ARCHER. You're in her debt, how you going to discharge it?

CHARLES. She's in here with her cute 'lil Chinese *baby,* and her *girlfriend,* Daisy.

ARCHER. You can't marry two women, Chuck. It's against the law.

CHARLES. If we got the Chief Justice to come down here. Like an "activist judge"…? They make the law…

ARCHER. Why would he do that?

CHARLES. If I threatened to show everyone "those tapes" of him on the party boat on Lake Winnipesauke…

ARCHER. The country. Will not vote for you, Chuck, *however* much airtime you buy. If you marry those women.

CHARLES. What about if it was "Opposite Day?"

ARCHER. "Opposite Day?"

CHARLES. Yeah.

ARCHER. It's not a legal holiday.

CHARLES. ...it's *not?*

ARCHER. No.

CHARLES. *Huh...*

(*pause*) And she's writing me this beautiful *speech...*

ARCHER. That's great.

CHARLES. No it's better than that, it's going to be my legacy.

ARCHER. Uh huh.

CHARLES. Because, you know what her and me have?

ARCHER. What do you have?

CHARLES. A dream.

ARCHER. You know when people have dreams, Chuck? When they're sleeping.

(**BERNSTEIN** *pokes her head in.*)

BERNSTEIN. Sir?

ARCHER. (*cont.*) Give us a minute.

(**BERNSTEIN** *exits.*)

(*to* **CHARLES**) Chuck: you want to be President for four more years?

CHARLES. (*pause*) I promised Bernstein.

ARCHER. I know that you did.

CHARLES. I *need* her.

ARCHER. Uh huh.

CHARLES. And I *owe* her...

ARCHER. Sometimes, Chuck...

CHARLES. Yes...

ARCHER. ...part of the burden of command...

CHARLES. Yes...

ARCHER. ...is you have to sell the other fellow out.

CHARLES. ...you have to sell the other fellow out.

ARCHER. Yes.

CHARLES. Uh huh…

ARCHER. For the "common good."

CHARLES. For the "common good."

ARCHER. Well. Now you're talking.

CHARLES. Cause, for the common "good," yeah, I could do it, but, uh…

ARCHER. That is because you're a moral man.

CHARLES. But, if it was just, uh…"expediency," I couldn't…

ARCHER. No, fuck that. *Fuck* that, Sir. We're speaking of the absolute integrity of That One Man, who occupies the Highest Office in the land. *(pause)* Who would like to *hold* the highest office in the land *(pause)* rather than go home and play pitch and putt golf with Cathy.

CHARLES. *(pause)* What do I do?

ARCHER. *(pause)* Here's what you do: We set the T.V. Cameras up. We introduce you, THE CAMERAS, HOWEVER, ARE *OFF*. We tell the T.V. Guys it is a matter of, uh… "National Security."

CHARLES. "National Security?"

ARCHER. What are they gonna say?

(The phone rings.)

(to phone) Yes, we're coming out.

*(**ARCHER** starts helping the President into his shirt, their backs are to the door as **BERNSTEIN** enters holding a bouquet, the Chinese amulet around her neck.)*

ARCHER. *(cont.)* The girls come on, you "marry" them. They "think" they have been married. She hands you your speech. Weep weep weep, they broom the broads, we turn the cameras on, you give the speech, and you pardon the turkeys.

CHARLES. But…

ARCHER. You can't marry those two women and win the election.

(pause) Is that right or not? Look me in the eyes.

CHARLES. That's right.

(They turn and see **BERNSTEIN** *standing there.)*

CHARLES. *(cont.)* Uh...

BERNSTEIN. I wanted to ask if you'd give me away.

CHARLES. *BERNSTEIN.*

(pause) Uh...

BERNSTEIN. And you're selling me out.

CHARLES. Bernstein, you know, I, um...

ARCHER. What the President is *doing...*

CHARLES. What I'm *doing*, Bernstein, is a...

ARCHER. ...it's a Strategic Re-Ordering of Priorities.

(pause)

CHARLES. Well, Bernstein...you know...

BERNSTEIN. What about the Shade Tree Mechanics...?

ARCHER. ...the "shade tree mechanics...?"

BERNSTEIN. Who built this country.

ARCHER. Were any of them lesbians?

BERNSTEIN. They may have been.

ARCHER. Why, because they were wearing coveralls...?

BERNSTEIN. ...sir.

CHARLES. Just because they were wearing *coveralls* Bernstein, does not mean they were lesbians.

ARCHER. That's right.

CHARLES. "Coveralls," in fact, were, curiously, once worn by "men."

ARCHER. That's right.

CHARLES. ...in the factories, and so on.

ARCHER. That's right.

CHARLES. Which once dotted our land.

ARCHER. ...read your *history...*

CHARLES. So, so, Bernstein...

ARCHER. Bernstein, there are Bigger Issues involved here...

BERNSTEIN. Oh, Sir, you have lowered yourself in my estimate.

CHARLES. Whoa whoa whoa whoa whoa: I'm gonna tell you what. Bernstein? You and your pal. Go home. One of you throw on a sportcoat, come back, *allow* the American Public to *infer* that one of you's a man, and on we go.

BERNSTEIN. Sir, my partner is a woman.

CHARLES. Who is to say what a woman is?

BERNSTEIN. Sir.

CHARLES. Many fine doctors...

BERNSTEIN. Sir.

CHARLES. Are unable, *totally*, at birth, to determine...

ARCHER. Absolutely.

BERNSTEIN. Mist...

CHARLES. ...the sex...uh...of the uh child.

ARCHER. Chucky...

CHARLES. Resulting in...

ARCHER. Chucky. I need you to clear your mind.

CHARLES. ...great, *great* sorrow, as the infant grapples...

ARCHER. Cause in two minutes you are going on international T.V.

CHARLES. ...in later life.

ARCHER. Chuck.

CHARLES. As the kid, in high school, trying out for *track*, *field* hockey for example, and, she finds out, she's a *guy*.

ARCHER. Sir...

CHARLES. *Opening* herself, to uh, uh, "hazing..."

ARCHER. Sir...?

CHARLES. *(pause)* Because of a simple error. On the uh, *birth* certificate, the fucken *nurse* checked off the wrong, uh...

ARCHER. Chuck.

CHARLES. Sex...

ARCHER. Chuck...

CHARLES. ...of the child.

BERNSTEIN. Sir, my partner is a woman.

CHARLES. Who are you to judge?

BERNSTEIN. I'm sure *she'd* say she is a woman.

CHARLES. At the cost of your happiness?

> *(pause)* I'm going to tell you, Bernstein, I don't care *what* sex she is. Couldn't care less. If she *merely...*

BERNSTEIN. She's wearing a wedding dress.

CHARLES. Allows it to be *inferred*, that she...

BERNSTEIN. Sir.

CHARLES. ...is *any one thing* but a woman, I will hitch you up so tight, your eyes will pop.

BERNSTEIN. Sir...

CHARLES. Well, then, do you know what? Fuck *you*. Because, this is the trouble with your liberal agenda.

BERNSTEIN. What is that?

> *(***TURKEY GUY*** enters.)*

TURKEY GUY. Sir, the cameras are about to roll. The turkeys are *restive*, and I assume you've resolved that other matter.

BERNSTEIN. What is the problem with my liberal agenda, Sir?

CHARLES. You are willing to sacrifice the happiness of actual flesh and blood "people" to protect some cockamamie, dumb idea of "Justice."

BERNSTEIN. I take the strongest exception to your speech.

CHARLES. And so you want to "Save the World."

TURKEY GUY. Uh, uh...

CHARLES. And all that happy horseshit.

BERNSTEIN. Sir...

CHARLES. But, not unless you and your pal can have a little piece of *paper...*

BERNSTEIN. That quote little piece of paper, as you denigrate it, is the symbol of our...

CHARLES. Oh, stuff a sock in it.

BERNSTEIN. HUMAN DIGNITY.

(sneezes)

CHARLES. Oh, please.

TURKEY GUY. Sir.

BERNSTEIN. We named our baby after you.

ARCHER. Bernstein: It's just, JUST not going to happen.

(pause)

BERNSTEIN. I wrote you such a beautiful speech…

CHARLES. I'm sorry, Bernstein…

BERNSTEIN. About how, as a nation, those things which *unite* us…

*(**BERNSTEIN** gives the speech to **CHARLES**.)*

*(to **CHARLES**)* …here…

(pause) Read it, Sir. The words are mine, but the ideas are yours.

*(The phone Rrings. **ARCHER** answers and listens.)*

ARCHER. Yes.

(hangs up the phone)

CHARLES. *(reads)* "The Little League, the *sewing* circle, the *scout* troop."

ARCHER. The turkeys died.

CHARLES. "our blessed American spirit of cooperation"

ARCHER. The turkeys are dead.

BERNSTEIN. I beg your pardon.

ARCHER. The turkeys are dead.

TURKEY GUY. No. No. The turkeys can't be dead.

(He takes the phone.)

What do you mean the turkeys are…

ARCHER. …what did they die of?

TURKEY GUY. *(to phone)* What did they… *BIRD FLU*?

CHARLES. Bird flu?

TURKEY GUY. *(to phone)* They died of Bird Flu…? HOW COULD THEY GET BIRD FLU, WE'VE HAD THEM IN AN ISOLATION TANK SINCE BIRTH…

CHARLES. *(to self)* ...the Fucken turkeys died of Bird Flu.

TURKEY GUY. *(to phone)* How...who, who, has anybody in the office been to *China*...

ARCHER. *(takes phone)* Okay, okay. ...*Who* said it was Bird Flu?

CHARLES. Who said it?

ARCHER. The guy from Walter Reed.

CHARLES. A "doctor"...?

ARCHER. Yes, a doctor.

CHARLES. Who did he say it to?

ARCHER. He said it on national TV.

CHARLES. ...well, *that* sucks...

ARCHER. The birds died on national TV, the doctor walked over, and said it was bird flu.

TURKEY GUY. NO NO NO NO NO...

CHARLES. What was the doctor doing there...?

TURKEY GUY. *(to self)* The turkeys died.

ARCHER. You sent for him because Bernstein was sneezing.

TURKEY GUY. She was sneezing, and the other girl was sneezing and... *WHAT IS THAT ABOUT YOUR NECK?*

CHARLES. An ancient Chinese amulet.

TURKEY GUY. Where did you *get* it?

BERNSTEIN. China.

CHARLES. Yeah, she just came back from China.

TURKEY GUY. *YOU'VE GIVEN MY TURKEYS BIRD FLU.* You've killed my turkeys.

(begins to weep)

CHARLES. Get him a fucken sedative.

(ARCHER walks TURKEY GUY to the door.)

ARCHER. Bernstein, you swine...

CHARLES. *(to self)* The turkeys are dead.

ARCHER. You traitor lesbian swine...

CHARLES. Can I pardon the turkeys, though dead?

ARCHER. *(He flips up her amulet in a gesture of disrespect.)* What have you done?

CHARLES. ...what has she done...

ARCHER. She's plunged this country into chaos.

CHARLES. Will anybody still give me some money?

(The TURKEY GUY *re-enters, obviously upset, and starts for the President.)*

TURKEY GUY. You've Killed my Fucken Turkeys!!!

(ARCHER drags the TURKEY GUY from the room.)

CHARLES. *(to phone)* Could somebody please find the Secret Service? For the Love of God.

(hangs up phone; to BERNSTEIN) You've plunged this country into chaos, Bernstein.

(ARCHER reenters.)

Was this your intent...?

ARCHER. ...and she's cost us the election...

CHARLES. Was this your intent? You've ground this country to a halt. JUST BECAUSE YOU HAD TO HAVE A LITTLE CHINESE BABY. YOU COULDN'T GET KNOCKED UP, IN THE BACKSEAT OF A CHEVY, NO. LIKE EVERY OTHER AMERICAN GIRL IN HISTORY. But, no, you've got to tritze off to "China" and bring back avian borne *bird flu,* that scourge which will destroy civilization as we know it.

BERNSTEIN. Sir...

CHARLES. I'm very disappointed in you...

(The phone rings.)

Hello. Cathy. Yes. It's *Bird flu.* But: they'll send a bus, to take us to the Hole in the Mountains...right Arch?

(CHARLES looks to ARCHER, who nods.)

ARCHER. If you win...

CHARLES. What?

ARCHER. You can stay in the Hole in the Mountain as long as you're President.

CHARLES. They take you to the Hole in the Mountains, as long as you're President…

They kick you out of the Hole in the Mountains, when you're *not* President?

ARCHER. That is correct.

CHARLES. That's cold.

(**DWIGHT GRACKLE** *bursts in holding a peace pipe.*)

DWIGHT GRACKLE. Where *is* he…?

CHARLES. Now who the fuck are *you?*

DWIGHT GRACKLE. Who the fuck am I? Who the fuck am I? Look HERE:

(*shows pass which hangs around his neck*) That's who *I* am. Who the fuck are *you?* Eurotrash.

CHARLES. I'm the President of the United States.

(**ARCHER** *looks at pass and translates for the President.*)

ARCHER. "Dwight Grackle."

CHARLES. You know what? …Where is my security?

ARCHER. (*looks at watch*) Coffee break.

CHARLES. …fucken civil service.

DWIGHT GRACKLE. Chief Dwight Grackle, the incarnation of "raven," the trickster, messenger of DOOM.

CHARLES. …would you see if there's anybody *out* there, who's got a gun…?

DWIGHT GRACKLE. Avenger of the Micmac Nation.

CHARLES. Or a "fire hatchet" or something…?

(*Phone rings.*)

DWIGHT GRACKLE. Fucken USURPER.

ARCHER. Calm down.

DWIGHT GRACKLE. Don't tell me to calm down, for I have come for *blood…*

CHARLES. (*to phone*) Cathy, I'll have to call you back.

DWIGHT GRACKLE. I have come to avenge a debt of honor. Honor, you colonialist prick, but *you…*

CHARLES. How'd you get in?

DWIGHT GRACKLE. I have a pass. Sir? I have a pass, as if I *needed* a pass.

CHARLES. ...everybody needs a pass. How'd he get a pass?

ARCHER. You told the gate to *give* him a pass.

DWIGHT GRACKLE. As if I *needed* a pass. To walk on this land. As if...

CHARLES. Well, you've *got* a pass, so what are you bitching about?

DWIGHT GRACKLE. You maligned me and my people.

CHARLES. Big deal.

DWIGHT GRACKLE. And I'm gonna cut your fucken heart out and eat it in front of your dying eyes.

CHARLES. Perhaps I spoke intemperately.

DWIGHT GRACKLE. Your curse can only be expunged by blood.

CHARLES. Hey, those are big words.

ARCHER. He called *you* one, you called *him* one...

DWIGHT GRACKLE. And he maligned the Treaty of Porcupine Cove.

CHARLES. *Archie...* believe we have a COPY OF THAT "treaty", out in the outer office, would you.

ARCHER. Abso...

(starts to leave)

DWIGHT GRACKLE. NOT SO FRIKKIN FAST. *And* he suggested my second wife be eaten by a walrus.

CHARLES. Well, I'm sure that was traumatic.
(to phone) ...is there anybody out there with a big "ruler" or a cricket bat...

DWIGHT GRACKLE. Too late.

CHARLES. I don't *think* so, Dwight – as I *see*, after everything is said and done, man that you are, you've brought the peace pipe.

DWIGHT GRACKLE. It's not a peace pipe, dickwad. It's a *blowpipe* fashioned from the never-cut first bough of the Rowan tree, wrapped with the hair of fifteen virgins.

CHARLES. That's swell...

DWIGHT GRACKLE. And here's the kicker, what is *this?* A poison dart, its point the tooth of a female otter, dipped in wolverine blood and fox semen.

CHARLES. ...can anybody find a cop...?

DWIGHT GRACKLE. And an irreversible plant-based toxin known only to the elders of my tribe. Prepare to die.

BERNSTEIN. Don't do it Dwight.

DWIGHT GRACKLE. He has watered the land with the blood of my tribe.

BERNSTEIN. No doubt. But Dwight...I'm going to ask you, Dwight, to listen to the voice of reason.

CHARLES. You listen to the voice of reason, Dwight.

DWIGHT GRACKLE. You stole my land with honeyed words.

BERNSTEIN. He didn't steal your land.

DWIGHT GRACKLE. His ancestors.

CHARLES. My ancestors came from Lithuania.

BERNSTEIN. His ancestors came from Lithuania, Dwight.

DWIGHT GRACKLE. The weapon, having been unsheathed, cries out for blood.

BERNSTEIN. No, you can re-sheathe the weapon, Dwight; no harm's been done- give it to me.

DWIGHT GRACKLE. Stand back...

BERNSTEIN. Give me the blowpipe, Dwight.

DWIGHT GRACKLE. Each of us owes the gods a death. Pay up, you chucklehead.

BERNSTEIN. Stop! He's the leader of the Free World!

(**DWIGHT** *puts the dart in the blowpipe and fires it.* **BERNSTEIN** *interposes herself between the assassin and the President. The dart hits her and she falls. A pause.*)

BERNSTEIN. Oh, gosh...

CHARLES. Bernstein...

(pause)

BERNSTEIN. Mister President...

CHARLES. Bernstein, don't die...

BERNSTEIN. Mister President...My partner...

CHARLES. Yes, Bernstein, yes.

BERNSTEIN. My partner and I.

CHARLES. Yes.

BERNSTEIN. We...

CHARLES. Bernstein...

BERNSTEIN. We were going to vote for you.

(She dies. A pause.)

CHARLES. *(to* **DWIGHT GRACKLE***)* You sonofabitch. *YOU JUST COST ME TWO VOTES!!!*

DWIGHT GRACKLE. Oh, jeez.

CHARLES. What have you done? With your war-like impulses.

DWIGHT GRACKLE. I'm just that sorry...

CHARLES. Everyone's about to die from Bird Flu, awaiting some word of consolation, from their President, and my speechwriter's dead.

ARCHER. *(pause)* Hey, life goes on...

CHARLES. She took a poison dart for me.

ARCHER. ...she's a true patriot.

(The phone rings. **ARCHER** *answers the phone.)*

CHARLES. *(to self)* She gave up her life for her country...

ARCHER. *(to phone)* What?

CHARLES. Just like the Hist'ry books. Wow.

ARCHER. *(pause)* What? Say that again, please. Thank you. *(hangs up)*

(pause) The turkeys *aren't* dead.

CHARLES. What...?

ARCHER. I beg your pardon, they *are* dead, but they didn't die of bird flu.

CHARLES. They're "dead," but they didn't die of bird flu?

ARCHER. No.

CHARLES. What did they die of?

ARCHER. They exploded.

CHARLES. They "exploded?"

ARCHER. The TV lights were too hot.

CHARLES. Yes…

ARCHER. And they're all over the walls. They blew up.

CHARLES. But it's *not* bird flu?

ARCHER. Wait wait wait wait *wait*: if it *were* bird flu, the voters would have to stay home. And you win.

CHARLES. …but it's *not* bird flu.

ARCHER. No. The lights or something were too hot, and they expanded…*(to phone)* Yep. We're going with "Bird flu…"

BERNSTEIN. *(again alive)*…but then people will be frightened.

ARCHER. They're gonna do just fine. Excuse me, why are you alive…?

CHARLES. Bernstein…?

BERNSTEIN. Sir?

CHARLES. Why are you alive.

DWIGHT GRACKLE. *(reflectively)* …the poison has never failed.

CHARLES. …why…?

DWIGHT GRACKLE. *(similarly)* How has the white woman survived?

ARCHER. Bernstein? How have you survived?

BERNSTEIN. Uh, I think the dart struck my amulet.

(**CHARLES** *examines* **BERNSTEIN.** *We see the poison dart stuck in the Chinese amulet.*)

CHARLES. The dart has struck her amulet. The Chinese amulet has saved her life.

(The phone rings.)

ARCHER. Yes.

CHARLES. *(to self)* Huh...

ARCHER. It's the Secret Service, they're back from their coffee break...

CHARLES. The Chinese amulet signifying "love" has saved her life...

(pause)

ARCHER. ...and "are you okay"???

CHARLES. Bernstein, you saved my life.

BERNSTEIN. I can't tell you how happy I am, Sir, to serve.

CHARLES. I betrayed you, and yet, you risked your life for me.

ARCHER. You had your life saved by a lesbian. Great. "In the midst of Bird flu..."

CHARLES. You risked your life for me, why?

BERNSTEIN. Sir, you're the President. The people voted for you.

CHARLES. They were mistaken.

BERNSTEIN. That's their right.

CHARLES. Bernstein, *you* know who I am – I'm just some guy in a suit.

BERNSTEIN. Sir, with respect? So were all the other guys who sat here.

CHARLES. What? George *Washington*?

BERNSTEIN. Guy-in-a-suit.

CHARLES. Abraham Lincoln?

BERNSTEIN. Guy in a suit.

CHARLES. Bernstein, Lincoln freed the slaves. *I* can't free the slaves.

BERNSTEIN. You could marry me and my partner.

(pause) It would be your legacy.

CHARLES. ...my legacy...

ARCHER. Chucky...

CHARLES. *(holds up a hand for quiet)*

> *(pause)* I always *felt* that I'd do something memorable –
> I just assumed it'd be getting impeached. Huh.
>
> *(pause)* Bernstein – wash your face – you're getting
> married.

ARCHER. It'll cost you the election.

CHARLES. Damn job's a pain in the ass. Too much stress. Too little opportunity for theft. I'm broke, I'm tired, and I'm going home.

BERNSTEIN. ...what will you *do*...?

CHARLES. I'll have Thanksgiving at the kitchen table, Bernstein. I'll sit out on my front porch, and I'll watch the sun go down...on a life of Public Service.

BERNSTEIN. Sir, may I kiss you...?

CHARLES. In the Oval Office...? Get the fuck out of here.

> Bernstein. Come on. I'm giving you away.

ARCHER. *(re: Dwight Grackle)* What about the Indian?

> *(pause)*

CHARLES. Oh, yes: *Dwight?* United for an instant in this accident called "time," our paths converged. Now we part, each to his own fate. I go to poverty, you go to torture and death. Farewell.

DWIGHT GRACKLE. Sir? Wyntcha just *pardon* me, give me Nantucket Island, you n' me'll build a casino.

> *(pause)*

CHARLES. *Jesus* I love this country.

END OF PLAY

ABOUT THE AUTHOR

DAVID MAMET is a dramatist, director, novelist, poet, and essayist. He has written the screenplays for more than twenty films, including *Heist, Spartan, House of Games, The Spanish Prisoner, The Winslow Boy, Wag the Dog,* and *The Verdict.* His more than twenty plays include *Oleanna, The Cryptogram, Speed-the-Plow, American Buffalo, Sexual Perversity in Chicago,* and the Pulitzer Prize–winning *Glengarry Glen Ross.* Born in Chicago in 1947, Mamet has taught at the Yale School of Drama, New York University, and Goddard College, and he lectures at the Atlantic Theater Company, of which he is a founding member.

Also by
David Mamet...

American Buffalo
Bobby Gould in Hell
The Cherry Orchard
Dark Pony
The Dissappearance of the Jews
Dramatic Sketches and Monologues
The Duck Variations
Edmond
The Frog Prince
Glengarry Glen Ross
Goldberg Street
Keep Your Pantheon
Lakeboat
A Life in the Theatre
The Luftmensch
Mr. Happiness
The Old Neighborhood
The Poet and the Rent
Reunion
The Sanctity of Marriage
School
The Shawl
Speed-the-Plow
Squirrels
The Water Engine
The Woods

Please visit our website **samuelfrench.com** for complete
descriptions and licensing information.

OTHER TITLES AVAILABLE FROM SAMUEL FRENCH

KEEP YOUR PANTHEON

David Mamet

Comedy / 11m

In *Keep Your Pantheon,* an impoverished acting company on the edge of eviction is offered a lucrative engagement. But through a series of riotous mishaps, the troupe finds its problems have actually multiplied, and that they are about to learn a new meaning for the term "dying on stage."